Conscious Culture:

A Game Plan to Build a Great Workplace

From grassroots to game plan, this book is the intersection of meaningful work, strong culture and you. Our template called the THRIVE™ Model encourages you to level-up your culture game (at work and home): helping today's leaders succeed in tomorrow's world. Unlike others books about workplace culture, we build on a heart-rooted foundation and utilize our model in order to grow. We believe in maximizing people – more than just making money – and then everyone wins. Together we THRIVE™.

Melanie Booher, BS, MHR, PHR, SHRM-CP

ISBN (978-0-578-90577-8)

Portions of this book are works of nonfiction. Certain names and identifying characteristics have been changed.

Front Cover Design by Vera Soper, ERA Designs

The THRIVE™ Model designed by Sara Uhlenbrock-Health

Printed by Amazon, in the USA

First Printing Edition 2021

Influencer Network Media (Publisher)

10663 Loveland-Madiera Rd.

Suite 170

Loveland, OH 45140

www.thrivewithmb.com

CONTENTS

Dedication

Authors write books – not moms who work too much and are continually searching for that elusive work/life balance thing. When would I find the time? But as time passes, I realize that I have things I'd like to share. I have aspirations to do more, be more and share more. Plus, this extrovert needed to fill some time during a pandemic. Boom just like that – a motivator and time finder.

I also want my kids to see the living and loving connection that can exist between work and life. How good people can make the world great – one small step at a time.

> *"It is not our job to toughen our children up to face a cruel and heartless world. It is our job to raise children who will make the world a little less cruel and heartless." – LR Knost*

And so, I dedicate this book to my family: my constant encouragement to do better. My dad who always believes in me. My mom who gave me a passion for games, a thirst for knowledge and my creative side. My kids who make me want to be a better person and live a life worthy of a legacy. My sister Megan – the perfect best friend that I didn't have to search for and never have to work to impress. My brother Greg who encourages me to be a better person with built in reminders to maintain my level of patience. And to my GG, cousins and the rest of our big Italian family, for the love and support you always provide.

Second, I dedicate this book to my colleagues, starting with my Miami University professor and friend Tom Mobley, who encouraged me to write the book in the first place. To my networking family (wish I could name you all – but especially Kathleen Crawford, Mark Allen, Katie Scanlon, Elisabeth Galperin, Nancy Piatt, Nanette Polito, Meghan Donnellon Hyden, Rob Apple, and Janelle Paynter) who support my entrepreneurial endeavors and have become amazing colleagues. To my HR & Culture mentors: my uncle Rocky Felice, Giuseppe Delena, Cheryl Cowan, Stacie

Webster, Anna Choi, Steve Van Valin, Geri Morgan, Jennifer Payne, Steve Browne, David Friedman, Alex Bowden, Colleen Pfaller and my SHRM and University of Cincinnati MHR colleagues, who all played an important role in helping me to evolve into an HR Professional, find my voice and make my dream a reality.

To those who helped me make this book a reality: Jodi Brandstetter, Sara Uhlenbrock, Melissa Saneholtz, Trisha Webb and Vera Soper. You are all rock stars in your own right. I am forever thankful.

To my friends: Nicole Kimble, Heather Blair, Rachael Ansar, Kelli Brown, my neighborhood of amazing friends and all those who have supported me throughout the years – you are the best support network a girl could ask for. I can only hope to pay it forward to all of you in the same way. I am so lucky to have such an amazing tribe.

Finally, I must thank my husband Matt for inspiring me to think differently, to stay the course, to think about the numbers more, to cuss because it feels good and it's not the worst bad habit to have, to find the joy of missing out (JOMO) instead of the fear of missing out (FOMO), to fly in the face of convention when needed. Without his support and love, I don't know where I would be.

Thank you my dear – I love you *really* much.

> *"Loving ourselves through the process of owning our story is the bravest thing you will ever do." – Brené Brown*

Introduction

It was one of the most important days of my career and a pivotal point for our organization's future – and he didn't show up.

Rewind to the fall of 2015, where I was fortunate to be part of a team invited to attend the Best Place to Work pep rally event at the Cintas Center at Xavier University, Cincinnati, OH. It was there that the "Aha" moment I needed to spur me into entrepreneurship happened.

After months of preparing for the big event and pep rally, the team was ready and excited to attend. Our leadership team granted everyone a half-day off (which is already a huge deal in most organizations but a really *major* accomplishment in a billable environment). Donning matching t-shirts, light up noise makers and orange pompoms in place – our hopes were aimed at winning. I felt like a kid at Christmas, and our team was so excited that you could feel the positivity like an electric charge throughout the arena.

However, on the morning of the event, the crack that I had been holding together with duct tape and dreams started to sever. It started with a text from our CEO in which he said that he would not be attending. "Are you ok? Is your mom ok? What's going on?" I grasped for an answer. The crack was getting bigger and bigger. And he casually replied, "Yeah, I'm fine. But this stuff is like kids' soccer. Everyone gets a prize. You go – I'm just *not* really into it."

Boom. The crack was now a gaping hole amid the foundation of what could have been an amazing leadership team. No matter how hard I worked to hold our workplace culture together, this was the ultimate smack in the face. I had never used this analogy before, but alas, I knew what it meant to "lead a man to water, but you cannot make him drink." I was shocked and saddened.

How would I explain this to the team without deflating their excitement? I knew that I could no longer continue providing the smoke and mirrors of a strong workplace culture anymore – if he wasn't on board to support it.

Regardless of his lack of attendance, the team showed up excited and ready to see what the day held for us. I could see the hint of disappointment when they asked where he was, so I reassured that something had come up and then quickly deflected toward the excitement of the day.

In a blur of pep rally cheering and announcements, we jumped out of our seats and began the sea of high fives and hugs when our name was announced as the winner for our size organization.

First place. Officially considered a "Best Place to Work."

Such a proud moment and yet also so very sad. It was a day of great success...and also great failure. Our CEO did not see the value of attending the event to support the (his) team, building into our strong culture. He didn't get to see the excitement of the team rallying and celebrating all that we had accomplished.

When we returned to the office that Monday, I offered him a high five. He looked at me strangely and said, "What's that for?" I was dumb struck. Really? We just won a huge award, and he couldn't ride that high for four days.

My heart ached for a do-over moment, but I knew it was time for me to go. This was the “Aha” moment that changed the course of my professional life. Our fundamental views about how businesses succeed (bringing people us with us, not stepping on their backs as you ventured upward) were just too different, and it was time for me to move on.

After a long and difficult discussion, where he initially asked me to stay - we planned my transition out of the company. Of course, I would go nicely (we didn’t want to hurt his ego or reputation among the team/community). We agreed to tell everyone that I was starting my own "Culture Coaching" company, and he assured me that he would be my first client. Yet, unsurprisingly, somehow that never quite worked out.

Regardless, I upheld my end of the agreement. I hired my replacement and trained her well. With a six-month transition timeframe, I worked my new idea on the side and secured three clients to launch my new business based on what I knew was a formula for success: Heart-Rooted (HR)

Leadership and creating Best Places to Work. And I have never looked back.

What an amazing ride it has been thus far! As a Culture Coach, I've helped five companies achieve "Best Place to Work" status and many more along the path of a stronger culture, worked with High Performing Culture (now CultureWise) to get Culture Coach certified, spoke at conferences, created *Cards for Culture©, The Business Edition* and had the privilege to work with leaders across the United States who truly believe their success comes from their people – developing strong and intentional cultures in Cincinnati and beyond.

Each year in the fall, a favorite photo resurfaces on Facebook, and the mix of memories (overwhelming joy and sadness) come flooding back. The photo shows 15 of my all-time favorite colleagues – so excited at our accomplishment. Wearing our matching shirts and huge smiles and proudly holding our pompoms high. The excitement is palpable. And there I am in the middle – glowing with excitement and proudly holding our Best Place to Work trophy. It's a favorite memory surrounded by some of my favorite colleagues of all time.

And, of course, an important person is missing from that photo. Someone who self-selected out and never bothered to show up. This story is a microcosm of what happens when leaders don't value people. The truth plays itself out. It's important to understand that only 4 out of 15 of those smiling faces are still employed at the company. A sad 26.67% retention rate of amazing people. Because good people don't continue working for leaders who don't appreciate them, who don't value people and culture and who don't show up on important days.

We shall use this story a launching point because while I'm very proud of what I've accomplished thus far, it's really just beginning.

I've gathered insights, knowledge and quotes from many of my favorite leaders, and you will see them throughout this book. Whether related to leadership, life, culture or business, there are a lot of strong leaders providing us with their wisdom. I've collected these over the years and worked quite a few into the book – I like to think of it as collective culture wisdom.

I've included some bonus personal material that I affectionately call "dad-isms." I can hear my dad saying, "I oughta write a book," (because he has so many stories and catch-phrases that have surfaced throughout my life) and "since the apple doesn't fall far from the tree," well dad, you don't have to write a book – I've got your back.

My father grew up in rural Kentucky. After Cumberland University, he went into teaching and gradually worked his way up the ladder within education: teacher and coach, athletic director, assistant principal and then principal. For many years, I thought that I'd follow in his footsteps. But dad knew the politics of education too well, and when he strongly encouraged me to take a different path at Miami University, I chose the school of business. At the time, I remember thinking that Human Resources was like teaching adults instead of kids. I'm thankful for the redirect, because I am very fortunate and happy to be where I am today.

Dad's words of wisdom often surface in my mind due to repetition throughout my life – like an ongoing song chorus. Some of them are quite funny, but they all possess layers of insight. I'm not 100% sure that my dad was the originator of all of them, but I have a hand-written journal of 214 sayings that I've collected over the years. Not all are appropriate for print, but they all make me think of him. So, cheers to dad! I'm putting a few to good use, and you will see them scattered throughout this book. Even though he is long retired from teaching, I appreciate these golden nuggets of wisdom. Thanks, dad, for being a life-long teacher.

Bottom line, I wanted to write this book because I truly believe that *everyone* deserves to work for an organization that they love, where they are treated well and feel valued, where they get to be their best self and enjoy coming to work every day and where success and profit happen because of a meaningful and reciprocal relationship.

My business motto for years has been, "When People Matter, Companies THRIVE™," and I truly believe that. But I've also come to realize how much bigger this mantra can be.

Conscious Culture speaks to the belief in bringing our whole self to the table during interactions, being self-aware and being intentional, positive, present and engaged. It's also important to recognize that there's an overlap in our professional and personal lives that cannot be ignored. *When we work to be a good person, we personally create a good workplace.* That goodness rubs off on others and is contagious. Society shines brighter when we embrace this truism of humanity – we just need to give it space to take root, nurture it and let it grow.

"Vulnerability is not winning or losing. It's having the courage to show up when you cannot control the outcome." - Brené Brown

(I love me some Brené Brown, and she's the guru of vulnerability.) This quote reminds us to show up and leave it all on the table, knowing we cannot control all the outcomes. There is a great amount of *vulnerability* in writing a book, but I'm putting it out there in the hope that it helps others.

In some way, I hope my words (candid, personal, sometimes unrefined, and usually hitting at the core) help renew the fire in all my HR and business colleagues who are fighting the good fight…trying to fit a 40-hour to-do list into a 24-hour day. As we raise our families, try to be a good people and work hard, let us also leave some room for us to make our mark on the world and leave a legacy. One good person at a time. One human moment at a time. Working our plan. Paying it forward. One conscious culture conversation at a time.

Hopefully by the end of this book you will have both inspiration and a plan to set in motion, and you will believe in your own ability to pay it forward.

Together we THRIVE™. Let me show you how...

PART I

1

CULTURE MATTERS (PROFESSIONALLY AND PERSONALLY)

There's no magic wand or crystal ball. And if you think that workplace culture is only about work, then herein lies the problem.

Our society is often obsessed with work, and it takes up a lot of our waking hours. But to really thrive in life, we must bring our *best selves* to the table every day – at home and at work. Examine our personal character, connection with others and values that make us successful and apply those to work.

People leave bad bosses, not companies. People also leave bad cultures (because it's the bad bosses that create those). I could have titled this book, "Jerk Cultures Don't Work" or some variation. The saddest part of that is that most of the jerks have their fingers pointed squarely at someone else. Of course, *they* are never the problem.

A side note about the title stuff: laughingly, I can hear my dad recommending, "Run Silent, Run Deep" as the title which was the title he suggested for *every* movie, book, song or anything that he forgot the actual title. And while cultures do run silent and deep, that sounds rather ominous. Since culture errs on the side of positive, I wanted to choose a title that reflected that too. And trust me, titles might be harder to choose than naming your children. The struggle was real. Another example of culture conversation arose just around the title alone, and we landed on something that felt good. Sorry, dad, not your first preference, I know. And if you cannot remember the title, just rely on your trusty fallback. I don't mind.

But back to bosses. All leaders (all people who work really) must embrace the importance of their role in creating a successful atmosphere where everyone (including the organization) can thrive. Whether you are the CEO, HR leader, customer service representative or maintenance person, you deserve a great workplace culture. And this book is for you.

If you are in a small business environment, you may have an easier time getting some of these ideas for culture change implemented. Get the ball rolling to make meaningful changes. As the key decision maker, take pride in knowing that you have the power to impact your entire team in a wonderful way.

If you are in a larger organization, you will certainly encounter more red tape. Don't be discouraged. Start small (within your team or department), start to have culture conversations of your own (guided by this book and your own knowledge about great workplace culture), build off of your current vision/values by determining how those come to life in your department and grow from there. Regardless of your role and/or the size of the organization, it's important to find your voice in order to create your desired culture and lead the organization to success.

Culture is not a buzz word. It's important to understand some of the background about workplace culture. It's so much more than just a buzz word. Buzz words come and go, but culture is here to stay. In fact, just like compensation, it's a workplace expectation.

After the challenges of 2020, it's a necessity. Still unsure? Here are some interesting and informative numbers from *Fast Company* magazine[1]:

- 66% of consumers consider elements like company culture and employee welfare as factors that determine whether they buy from one brand over another

- Replacing an employee costs up to 150% of their annual salary and drives productivity into the ground

- 77% of people would consider a company's culture before applying for a job there

- Nearly 80% of Americans say they expect a company's leadership to support racial equality

While this book has a focus on organizations, there is also a very personal application that occurs here also. Amazing cultures don't start on their own through spontaneous combustion; they are the result of good people putting in the work. Your personal values, character and style show up at work. Throughout this book you will see both the personal and professional sides of what I have learned about this process manifested in different ways.

I started my business as an entrepreneur and mom of three who was tired of bad bosses, corporate America BS and too many hours spent away from loved ones. If I was going to spend *endless* hours dedicated to my work and away from my family, well, dang it, I wanted to enjoy that work time! I was certain that other parents (anyone working, really) had to feel the same heart pangs when pulled to work. This desire fueled me for more than just myself; I wanted to impact others' lives for the better, too.

When my daughter Madilynn brought home the book, *Pay It Forward* by Catherine Ryan Hyde[2], the wording immediately caught my attention. At first, Madi and I started taking turns reading (she's my kid who struggles a bit in this area); however, what started as a bit of a homework chore turned into genuine bonding time that we looked forward to each evening. Others in the family took interest, and slowly but surely, the number of readers increased. Eventually, it included the whole family looking forward to and reading the book together every night – all five of us huddled together, passing the book and taking turns reading. A good family moment to remember for sure.

I love the premise of the book: Trevor takes his extra-credit school assignment "THINK OF AN IDEA FOR WORLD CHANGE AND PUT IT INTO

ACTION" and turns it into a vast movement of kindness and goodwill spreading around the world. The idea was simple: do a profound good deed for three people and ask them each to "pay it forward" to three others who need help. And so, the exponential goodness spreads. *Pay It Forward* has become a movement that has changed lives around the world.

It's with that kind of enthusiasm and passion that I often talk about workplace culture and the THRIVE™ Model. It's a big dream and even bigger goal, but it's what I truly hope could happen. Imagine the momentum of a few strong leaders, building their culture and creating a few great places to work. All of those employees are positively impacted. And they have families and loved ones who they go home to at night where they are happier, more engaged and more connected. The snowball effect amplifies, and the positivity is contagious. And it grows. All starting with how we embrace the day ahead of us and the choice we make to improve ourselves and our work culture. What do we choose to be known for? What kind of legacy do we want to leave behind?

I don't want my tombstone to someday read: "Melanie – she was a great employee who followed all the rules." I'd much prefer it to say something like, "She challenged status quo, sharing her vision of great culture to help others survive and thrive and trying to make life better for humankind." It's a tall order – I get it. But it's my "why." It fuels my passion, helping others along the way and lifting them as I go.

> *"If you want to lift yourself up, lift up someone else." – Booker T. Washington*

Ask yourself this question: Is personal improvement a biproduct of the professional work that we are doing or vice versa? Does our work make us better people? Do we make our workplace better because we are in it?

I believe that good people create great workplace cultures. If you have a wonderful workplace and hire someone who is not a good person, sooner or later you will know it. Can that person change and assimilate? Maybe, but not likely. People are products of history and past behaviors. For example, if a person doesn't have the ethics you desire for your team, it will be difficult to teach him/her those acceptable ethics and how to stand by them at all costs. You are re-wiring years of what was deemed acceptable behavior. It's far easier to set the expectation for what good ethics and values mean within your organization and hire people who naturally fit that mold.

> *"Empathy is about standing in someone else's shoes, feeling with his/her heart, seeing with his/her eyes. Not only is empathy hard to outsource or automate, but it makes the world a better place." – Daniel Pink*

Leading with heart is something that not everyone is prepared to do, yet I believe everyone could do it with a change in mentality and a simple plan for action. The first step: shift your mindset to one that truly believes we all deserve to enjoy our work and work environment. Then start to build a plan and develop specific actions that will lead toward this improvement. Then the snowball is rolling... and each person we are able to pull into this idea will help us grow it exponentially.

2

EXPERIENCE AND HISTORY

I have 20+ years of Human Resource and business experience at a variety of organizations (big and small) in multiple industries (light manufacturing, retail, banking, marketing, design and engineering...just to name a few).

I obtained my Bachelors' Degree in Human Resources and Organizational Development from Miami University and a Masters in HR from the University of Cincinnati. I've gained meaningful and applicable experience working for powerhouses like Macy's, Cintas, Provident Bank and Charming Shoppes. After working in the corporate world for 12 years, I wanted to try my hand in small/mid-sized businesses and worked for a marketing firm and design company.

Every job prepared me for the next, and interestingly, I enjoyed each one more than the last. However, I did feel this growing urge to have more control over my work and schedule. I wanted to figure out what the elusive "work/life balance" really was (I don't know if I ever found it really), so I decided to start my own business in the fall of 2015.

I've been running my HR and Culture Consultancy since then and loving it. Expanding my reach so that I can help other leaders and their organizations build a great workplace culture has felt so good. In 2019, I took the extra step to get certified as a Culture Coach. All of this knowledge building and experience led to the creation of this book and a new innovation to gamify culture called *Cards for Culture©*. I'm thrilled to pull together all these experiences and share them with others. Truly making culture a little more tangible and putting it in willing hands.

This book is a labor of love, gathering my experience and organizing it into a way that makes sense for you. Many leaders have commented that the THRIVE™ Model helped them take all their ideas and organize them into a system that is trackable and provides them with a checklist and structured approach to attack each area of importance. I hope you can use it in the same way.

Over the years, I helped organizations become a "Best Place to Work" by instilling big-company best practices within an entrepreneurial environment. Rooted in my experiences as a people connector, change agent and business coach, my passion is driving organizations to truly *live* their values, not just post them on the conference room walls.

My favorite work projects often surface as things like:

- Culture Strengthening and Discussions
- Leadership Development & Coaching
- Fractional HR and Recruitment
- Diversity Equity and Inclusion Programs
- Leveling-up your People Operations/HR
- Speaking Engagements

Of course, I owe a great deal to all the mentors and leaders who have helped shape my views over the years, and for that I am forever thankful.

One such leader is David Friedman with CultureWise (formerly High Performing Culture/HPC). The THRIVE™ Model was created before I knew David, but some of my favorite culture knowledge comes from his teachings and books, *Fundamentally Different*[3]and *Culture by Design*[4]. I highly recommend that you read these books to support your own culture journey. His team also has an app that's rather amazing and worth checking out if your team is tech savvy and into apps. Thank you, David, for your insights and work in the culture world – you and your team are furthering the cause to ensure culture matters and workplaces are great.

HPC sited five top reasons why world-class organizations make working on their culture a strategic priority:

- To stand out and win business
- To find and keep A-level talent
- To execute at higher levels
- To protect the existing strong culture
- To preserve the founders' legacy

I'm impressed by HPC's work, and they are driving change at a national level. You can be part of it (see Partnership Links at the end of the book), too.

A significant differentiator between my work and HPC revolves around my desire to instill *customized the processes* along the way. Scalable is good because you can reach more organizations. But I wanted my work to be felt at the personal level, to see results so that people love work more. Then factoring in my culture background and experience as we instill HR elements as the main habit drivers.

I do this by holding meaningful culture conversations, gamifying leadership discussions (*Cards for Culture©),* utilizing a creative yet organized plan to provide structure (the THRIVE™ Model), creating an option for leaders to do this yourself (by getting certified as a Culture Coach) and providing additional support where needed (the THRIVE™ Collective – a group of subject matter experts who can help with strategic or tactical projects as needed).

My skills and desire seem best suited for the small/mid-market, helping where the rubber meets the road. Coaching leaders, holding accountable, facilitating culture conversations, creating and working our culture plan and building people-process habits for culture success (HR stuff!). However, all of this knowledge can be applied within any size organization within departments and teams. Since culture is *felt* at the team level.

As we have more and more culture conversations, my team repeatedly hears the need for improved culture. Layer in societal challenges (like those we faced in 2020 – pandemic, societal unrest, political upheaval and remote work and schooling) and workplace culture becomes even more critical. Do challenging times impact culture? Absolutely. Before, during and after. And now more than ever - culture is under the microscope.

During a great discussion with my colleague and friend Steve Browne, we agreed that people come together during a crisis, but we want to help them come together on a regular basis. Giving process and depth to culture and ensuring we have strong habits so that when chaos ensues, we can stay the course of doing the right thing (which would already be embedded in our process and would happen as a form of muscle memory because "that's just how we do business around here").

> *"During the pandemic, people rallied over the common bond, but what is that common bond going forward? Do we need the world the world to fall apart again to work together effectively? Wouldn't it be great for people to rally all the time, regardless of the situation?" – Steve Browne*

The purpose of this book is quite simple: to help leaders understand the importance of their most important asset – their people – and rally their people around aligned values and habits. I'll share with you why we need to be more intentionally focused on culture, outline a plan to improve and point you to resources, ideas and strategic interventions that will help you design an intentional culture strategy of your own.

"We must realize – and act on the realization – that if we try to focus on everything, we focus on nothing." — *John Doerr, Measure What Matters*[5]

Culture Matters. Company culture can be defined as the values and behaviors that are displayed within an organization, which determine the ways things get done. Good news: every company has a culture. Bad news: most leaders think they can create a best-in-class culture by trusting their gut and thus rarely create a strategic plan to guide them. NEWS FLASH: an amazing culture takes *intentional* effort (with ongoing leadership attention) and develops gradually over time. Culture is not a one-hit wonder.

Assess your organizational culture and customize a Culture Strategy with an ongoing purpose that ensures your people matter just as much (and even more) as your financial statement. When done correctly, your people can drive those financial forecasts through the roof. That's our vision: "When people matter, companies THRIVE™!" And we know that success follows those who adopt this people-first vision.

There's no quick and easy path; real effort is required. The weary need not apply. Roll-up your sleeves and put in the time. Leaders cannot shy away. We must have the difficult discussions (and the positive ones) and plan for the results that we desire. *We get what we work for – not what we wish for*. Therefore, it's important to stay the course, create your plan and work it. One step forward at a time.

"They day we plant the seed is not the same day we enjoy the fruit." – Hello Lovely Studios

3

HOW TO USE THIS BOOK

To maintain our focus, this book has six main sections based on the THRIVE™ Model, which help define areas of need. Each section focuses on a key area that really matters when dealing with organizational culture and includes: hiring the best *talent*, mitigating risk with maintained business *health*, *retention (recognizing* and *rewarding)* of employees, continually fostering *improvement* of processes, instilling company *vision* and *values* that teammates live by (not just posting it on the conference room wall) and ensuring that leaders are *engaged* and moving the enterprise forward in a meaningful way.

This book pulls together a culmination of years of experience, personal situations, countless seminars, books, articles, business coaches, life experience, favorite quotes, professional certifications, client relationships and more.

Beyond the acronym THRIVE™ and explanation of what each letter stands for, chapters include additional insights and ideas to drive culture change, personal applications and some stories that support the journey.

I recommend using the THRIVE™ Model as a heat map. This chapter includes a photo of the model, but you can also print one out at www.thrivewithmb.com.

To get started, simply circle the items that need additional attention and work, then check off the items that you feel good about or have completed. Be open to blind spots that will come into view. It's important to address those as they arise. Look for new ways to do things and get help when you need it.

In fact, very few people have the expertise to handle all of the areas on the THRIVE™ model. I recommend utilizing subject-matter-experts for areas that are not your core strength. This is not a time to get protective of turf or to let insecurity get in the way of progress. Instead, this is an ideal time to obtain fractional help to get some of these projects accomplished.

The best leaders surround themselves with people who are smarter than they are. They guide the strategic plan and allow others to contribute their expertise, and the leader can bask in the glory and come out looking like a superstar.

If budget doesn't allow for consultants to help with the project, find a consultant who will mentor/coach on a monthly/quarterly basis, teaching you to handle these projects on your own but providing structure and accountability. There will still be cost incurred, but it will be much lower. Still getting the job done. Brilliant.

Another option to consider: we have created a culture certification for those HR Leaders and Consultants who wish to learn how to THRIVE™ themselves. They are the THRIVERS – that's our name for this elite group of people who help others in achieving culture success. We want to spread the joy of strong culture to as many heart-rooted leaders as possible and teach them the ins/outs of what we have learned along the way. We have an entire tribe of culture coaches who are excited to share their knowledge and create more best-place-to-work cultures. If earning a culture certification is something that you have considered or sounds of interest to you, check out the Connect with Us section at the end of the book for more information.

As you continue to work your way through the book, it's critically important to stop and reflect on how you can apply the THRIVE™ Model to your workplace. Therefore, at the end of each chapter you will find a

Reflection Page to help you think through where you might *start, stop or continue* your efforts related to that section. This time of reflection is part of the intentional nature, so do it with purpose! Please use these pages to write down key actions and ideas.

Remember: taking notes helps us *remember things better* and *drive toward results*, and our culture success depends on both of those things.

At the end of the book, we added a section for Partnerships (professional recommendations) and Links. These friends/colleagues are all people who I highly recommend to help with your work on culture projects. It's a starting point if you need it – so be sure to check it out!

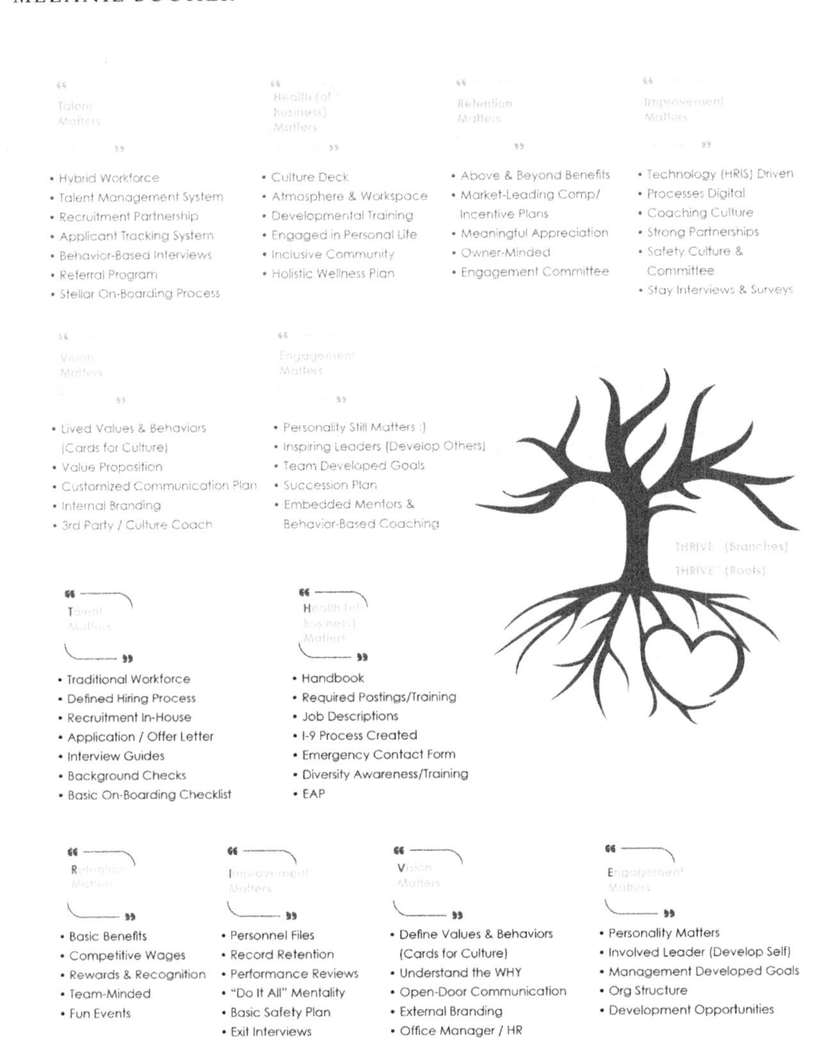

Get your printable version at www.thrivewithmb.com.

PART II

What does THRIVE™ stand for? Let's explore each letter.

4

TALENT MATTERS

THRIVE™ Model usage – TALENT MATTERS:

Start at the foundation/roots, ensuring that we meet the basic needs of a solid hiring plan, which includes:

• *Traditional Workforce:* Beginning as the baseline for where employers get started. It often can include very set hours like a Monday through Friday 8:00 am to 5:00pm. The employer provides all of the materials and supplies needed to do the job and typically the work is done onsite at the employers' location. The focus is on getting the work done, with little thought given to flexibility and innovation. Traditional organizations are very focused on the THRIVE™ roots / foundation and occasionally delve into the branches.

• *Defined Hiring Process:* Getting the right people on the bus really matters within an organization and setting the stage for how this happens is key. Create a repeatable process for recruitment: complete with job posting and weeding-out process, interview guidelines and progression and a new-hire checklist.

. . .

• *Recruitment In-House:* Recruiting needs to occur, and whoever can help is tasked with making it happen. There might be a dedicated employee who handles recruitment, but outsourcing and creative partnerships are not pursued.

• *Application/Offer Letter:* Ensuring that you are prepared for candidates and ready to make an offer is very important. Additionally, there are some important legal elements that should be included in the employment application. Your offer letter should be warm, engaging and complete with details like start date, job title, compensation, supervisor, location, vacation and benefit information.

• *Interview Guides:* Creating interview guides saves time, focuses the interview and guides your interviewers toward job appropriate questions. Ideally these guides are also aligned with organizational Vision and Values so that interviewers are not trusting their gut on whether the candidate is a culture fit.

• *Background Checks:* Checking into prior criminal history and employment experience of candidates in order to ensure basic safety for your team and to avoid neglect in hiring claims for your organization.

• *Basic On-Boarding Checklist:* Creating consistency as you bring on new employees is key to ensuring new hire success. Ensure you have a checklist that includes all of the pre-employment paperwork, technology and systems preparation and desk space are ready for our new teammates. This is not only a matter of efficiency, but also important in welcoming the new person in an organized fashion so that nothing falls through the cracks.

. . .

Once you have this foundation, you can move upward into the growth opportunities/branches:

• *Hybrid Workforce:* Adopting a more progressive style within the organization, in order to practice flexibility and innovation. You take a "bend and not break" approach in order to retain employees. This may manifest itself in creating more flexible work schedules, allowing employees to blend work- from-home and in-the-office time, with options for working less traditional hours (as long as the work gets done). This type of organization focuses on creative ways to accomplish work (digital prowess is high, they adopt a "let's try it and see how it goes" mentality). They desire engaged employees who are willing to run through walls for the organization- and seek to provide meaningful work, rewards and praise for employees. Hybrids adopt a THRIVE™ branches approach - wanting to ensure they level up their game in all aspects.

• *Talent Management System:* Moving beyond the paper files created from your hiring process and transactional processing, your organization desires to provide strategic assistance with an integrated software that improves processes related to recruitment, performance management, learning and development, and compensation management. There are a multitude of organizations that provide this service, so it's important to do you research and find one that works well for your needs.

• *Recruitment Partnerships:* Creating partnerships to supplement your hiring is helpful to your team and ensures that you are getting the best candidates possible. This allows experts to proactively seek talent, not just review passive candidates typically gained through job postings.

• *Applicant Tracking System:* Implementing technology enhancements to organize your paper applications and allow digital handling and tracking of recruitment and hiring needs. This is a central repository and database to improve hiring efforts and automate the process.

• *Referral Program:* Moving beyond the background checks (those are still needed), now the organization has created a referral program that pays employees a significant amount (enough to make us a little uncomfortable) for referring friends, family and colleagues into roles within our organization. Leaders are engaged in the hiring process at the right time in order to make the hiring process more robust and help new employees see how important getting the right people on the bus is to the entire team.

• *Stellar On-Boarding Process:* Moving beyond a basic on-boarding checklist into a more robust and stellar on-boarding experience. Engaging new employees from the beginning is critical for retention efforts, leading to higher job satisfaction, job performance, and organizational commitment.

When we do these things, we ensure that the *TALENT within* our business matters. We are building a foundation, making important choices, working our plan, engaging in strong habits to become a great place to work and leaving a culture legacy that will make us proud. When people matter, cultures THRIVE™.

> *"We don't hire smart people to tell them what to do. We hire smart people so they can tell us what to do." —Steve Jobs*

Great organizations know that talent (people) is the lynchpin for their success. Leaders often say that "people are our most important asset." However, when we dig deeper and ask how that rings true throughout the organization, there's little done to back that statement up. There's no strategy or plan related to people/culture. Would a CEO operate the business without a financial plan or accountant? Or without a marketing plan to grow the brand?

At a recent CEO Awards Event in Cincinnati, I heard these magical words spoken by the winning CEO as he was recognized on stage: "Top leaders ensure their organization operates with a solid financial plan, defined marketing initiatives, *and* they are intentional in developing a people/culture plan." This leader knows that his People Plan is a competitive advantage that sets his organization above the rest. He truly believes that people are his most important asset (not just the common phrase), and he is intentional about working a documented and strategic culture plan. Because of this, his business is thriving.

We are simply asking leaders to do more than trust their gut and create a plan that makes people a priority. We cannot hope for the best, hope for great employees or hope for business success. No. No. No. Hope is not a strategy.

> *"I used to believe that culture was 'soft,' and had little bearing on our bottom line. What I believe today is that our culture has everything to do with our bottom line, now and into the future." – Vern Dosch, author, Wired Differently*[6]

My colleagues at HPC conducted a survey of over 200 CEOs, asking: "How important are people/culture toward driving your bottom line?" and asking them to rate importance on a scale of 1-5 (1 being low/not important and 5 being high/very important). This was not soft stuff or fluff (feels good, morale boosting, etc.) but rather *bottom-line results*. People and culture driving the bottom line. I've replicated this survey to confirm the results among my own network of leaders and, of course, the results are similar each and every time. Also, my culture conversations with leaders are always enlightening for the leader, and trend down the same path.

I'm proud to report that the average score was very high (4.8). Put another way, 96% of leaders absolutely believe people/culture have a direct impact on the bottom line.

Next, the CEOs answered questions about whether they utilize a financial plan

(100% did) and/or marketing plan (95% had this). And the kicker: How many of you have a people/culture *plan*? Any guesses on the number here?

Less than 10%. Read that again. Yep, less than 10% had a written/intentional plan for their people/culture. As smart leaders and businesspeople are, we can see the issue here. We recognize that people/culture are critically important to impacting the bottom line (96%), but less than 10% have a plan to support this key element for success.

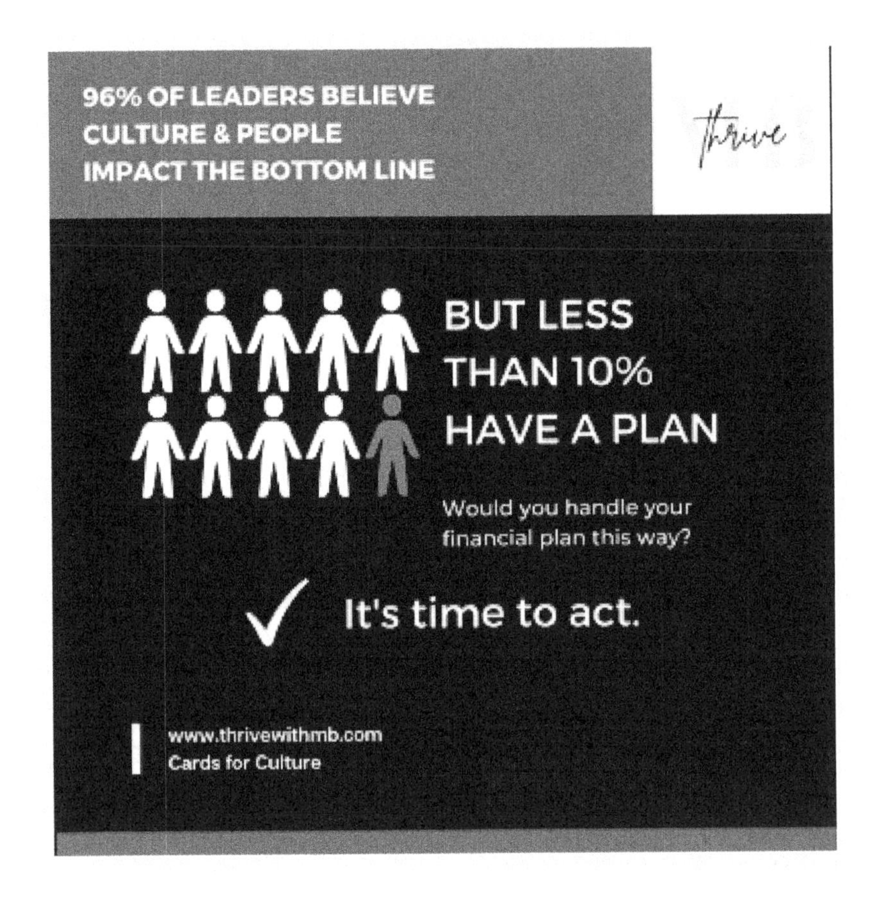

Put in other terms, 100% of CEOs value financials within the organization, and thus create a plan for success. What would happen if they just trust their gut or hope for the best related to financials? Would they dare not implement a plan?

This same logic *must apply* in order to bridge the gap between what we say matters (people drive our business profit) and the lack of planning. Leaving it up to chance, trusting our gut and/or hoping for the best simply is not a good business strategy.

If people are the foundation of a culture, the make-up of your team is essential. This is even more important in small business where you cannot hide a bad employee. You must ensure that the right people are on the bus. This analogy is critical since the bus is heading one direction with a limited number of seats.

There's an important adage: "Those with whom we surround ourselves most, represent who we are." Which reminds us to choose our team wisely. As we work to build our intentions around culture, we should also incorporate this into our hiring, coaching and performance processes so that our people align with the makeup of our desired culture. Every piece (person) builds into the whole (organization).

When I partnered with HPC in 2019, I learned a great deal about why culture matters, and I enthusiastically applied it to the THRIVE™ Model. We were speaking the same language in so many ways, but I could not set aside my HR lenses. We had amazing research on culture, and I absolutely thank them for sharing it with the world. I want to help spread the news. We cannot sit idly by planning for financials and not give our culture and people plans the level of attention they deserve.

However, more than just helping organizations set up their culture strategy, I also wanted to be around for the aftermath. After we define and discuss habits, who is in the trenches driving businesses to improve their people operations / human resource practices in order to get better? We were running with the ball as we defined the organizational culture, creeping closer and closer toward the goal line. The real magic exists in the strength of creating the habits that will be seen over and over within the organization. Those habits push the amazing culture work over the goal line. Furthermore, I wanted to stick around for the team high-fives and touchdown celebrations. Seeing those ongoing long-term successes is what sets up an organization for continued success. We cannot simply set up the plan; we have to see it through to fruition.

That next piece needed is HR leadership (people leadership). It was screaming for additional attention. And as a huge proponent of HR, I knew that habits related to HR were critical for people/culture success. I knew that I could apply all my HR knowledge and experience to help organizations create better habits (tell them how and work them into all the aspects of HR within organizations). If this meant supplementing with additional project work, training, coaching or consulting to see it through, that's what I wanted. Seeing value-based processes within people/HR processes – that's the key to success.

The good news was that my THRIVE™ Model stood out as the most obvious way to make this happen. My recipe for building great workplace cultures over and over again works, and that's the basis for this book. Culture Matters. Define it. Create habits. Ensure you are following a People Plan (THRIVE™ Model) and work that plan over and over. Don't let it sit on the shelf and get dusty. You and your people deserve better than that.

Seeing the results of all the hard work. Boom. That's the touchdown celebration that we all yearn to see!

> *"One piece of log creates a small fire, adequate to warm you up, add just a few more pieces to blast an immense bonfire, large enough to warm up your entire circle of friends; needless to say, that individuality counts but teamwork dynamites."* – *Jin Kwon*

Once the culture is fully defined and we know what we stand for, then we must take a look at our core business practices related to people (HR/People Operations) practices and apply them.

Those core practices included things such as hiring the best talent, onboarding with strong processes, living your vision/values, leading with habits to drive process and working fiercely to retain people. Yes, that's how you show that talent (your people) really matters and drives organizational health and success.

Our culture is only as good as our people; it's important the right people are on the team, and that means you must be very critical in looking at your hiring/recruitment processes. Culture is a multiplier, so we must invest time and energy into getting these processes right and filling the bus with the right people. Take time to review your processes and ensure they align with your culture.

Organizations with culture alignment should be asking interview questions related to the company's values (we call them Keys to Success). A good interview will combine behavior-based interviewing (ask very specific action-based interview questions in which past behavior will predict future behavior) with your company values. As an example, if delivering great customer service is paramount to your open position, you might ask candidates this question: "Tell me about a time that you delivered extraordinary customer service. What did you do? What was the result?"

This is very different from asking a question where the candidate can paint a picture to be anything that they want it to be, such as, "Tell me about your customer service skills?" Or "How do you define great customer service?" While those questions are ok, they do not get to the *root behavior* that this candidate *has actually performed in the past*, which is exactly what we want. We need to know that delivering great customer service is part of this person's regular habits (repeatable behavior) and built into their core – it's on autopilot, engrained in them and how they show up each and every day.

It's also important to remember that the candidates are interviewing you, too. There are many job options they could pursue, so why should they join your team? Ensure that your organization is looking at the internal/employee experience under the same microscope as the external/customer experience. This reciprocal relationship matters tremendously. Employees are not willing to settle on their happiness at work, and they will move on if a strong foundation, thriving culture and respectful leaders are not present.

Richard Branson once famously said, "Take care of your employees, and they'll take care of your business." His words of wisdom emphasize the importance of engaging your customers to engage your workforce. Organizations cannot afford a costly misstep here. Your hiring team/recruiters (anyone who is part of the hiring process) must put the best foot forward to recognize and appeal to the level of talent you are hoping to secure.

With that in mind, it's also critical to remember that not all people are "talent". Or at least, not the talent that you desire within your organization. Some you are better off without. If/when you realize that someone is not a good fit for your culture, it's important to take action to remove them (hopefully it's early enough and part of the interviewing process, but if they are already on the team, it still needs to be addressed).

Strong leaders know that it's important to not ignore or simply move the problem to another department, but actually let them go and doing our due diligence of coaching, listening and setting expectations if needed. But take pride in the idea of addition by subtraction – where your team actually gets stronger with the removal of a bad apple. Pluck the apple off the tree and keep moving. This solidifies your team's resolve and ensures you will continue to thrive.

> *"When people are financially invested, they want a return. When people are emotionally invested, they want to contribute." – Simon Sinek*

Ahh contributors – we want those. We desire emotional investment from our people, and we can create that when we define and align the culture. Our team will understand how to contribute. (That's why we defined the culture in the first place - to get everyone on the same page!) We are creating meaningful connection for our team. Treat people as more than just a number or a cog in the wheel; they are valuable contributors to the cause.

What's really interesting is that contribution is a measure of success and value to the business that is not as easily monetized as a financial investment. And that's ok. Many people don't have a ton of money to invest in your organization, but they do have their time and skills. Time, treasure, talent – sure we'd like to have all three, but don't underestimate how important time and talent are for your organization. When we invest in those, we create our own treasure.

> *"If you hire people just because they can do a job, they'll work for your money. But if you hire people who believe what you believe, they'll work for you with blood, sweat, and tears."* – Simon Sinek

A Story about Talent: Learning from Terminations

I've probably fired about 200 people in my lifetime – give or take a few. Usually, termination discussions went as well as they could, and a respectful conversation ensued. On the rare occasion that someone flew off the handle, it usually led to an interesting story.

I don't remember why we were terminating Johnny (which means it was probably something routine like attendance, disconnecting on a customer or related to poor performance). However, I do recall his intense exit.

Johnny was a big man and known to sometimes be hot tempered and disrespectful to coworkers. When he entered the interview room to start our discussion, he shifted his chair off to the side of the desk so that he was blocking the door. The only exit. I felt my palms starting to get sweaty as our conversation progressed, and Johnny started to get visibly upset. I wasn't sure why I was handling this without a witness (maybe everyone was busy at the moment), but being alone with Johnny was not a good choice.

I casually snuck my hand under the desk and pressed the panic button, hoping that it would work. See, we only recently had these installed in each of the interview rooms, and to my knowledge, no one had ever tried them out. Geeze, why did I have to be the guinea pig? My boss came to check on the situation and asked Johnny to calm down a moment, and then she had a colleague join us as a safety measure.

Johnny was really upset, and his temper flared. It didn't take long before he was yelling and causing a scene as we escorted him toward the lobby. We didn't typically have eventful terminations, but Johnny was in rare form. Everyone we passed on the way was quietly moving aside, casting knowing glances of what was happening and not wanting to get caught in the crossfire.

As we passed the front desk, Johnny continued to spew hatred, curse words and unforgettably called us the grossly inappropriate "c-word" as he karate-kicked the double doors and exited in grand fashion. My colleague and I looked at each other in awe. The front desk team and other employees in the lobby were speechless, staring our way in disbelief of what they just witnessed. That just happened.

I recall glancing around the frozen room and letting out a little giggle due to the discomfort of the inappropriate comedy that had just unfolded before us. The giggle was all that was needed to break the ice – everyone else started laughing a bit too. And just like in the movies, the lobby returned to its normal hustle and bustle; back to business as usual.

Needless to say, when the Unemployment Commission asked about Johnny's termination, we were happy to provide a photo of Johnny's award-winning, karate-kick exit (secured from our security cameras) with documentation and a nice write-up of his colorful words upon departure. The Unemployment Commission was not impressed, and his claim was denied.

I couldn't help but think that Johnny was never taught the value of catching more bees with honey or how to handle negative feedback with composure and grace. Behavior matters, and even as you exit an organization, one should practice some semblance of self-composure and respect. Burning a bridge is never a good idea, and kicking the bridge down isn't a good idea either.

Most terminations aren't quite this memorable. My colleague and I learned an important lesson in supporting others through difficult times and finding humor even in tough situations. We also recognized the importance of ensuring the right people are on our bus going forward. We had heard stories about Johnny's temperament and disrespectful nature, and it's very likely that Johnny had long outstayed his welcome and the leaders were ignoring a bad situation, likely walking on glass and trying not to poke the beast.

Can you imagine this kind of disrespectful behavior happening among the team on a regular basis? As we build our strong cultures, we must ensure teammates are displaying the behaviors that we want to see repeated and always nip poor or dysfunctional behaviors in the bud. We should promote, demote, realign and terminate based on this; addition by subtraction can be a good thing, and Johnny is a prime example of that.

***Personal Application*:**

Just as we apply the THRIVE™ Model to our business, we can apply these areas to our personal life as well. How does talent (people) show up regularly in our personal life?

It's important to think about our own personal characteristics and talents we possess in life, as well as what people we allow into our lives. If we are a reflection of those people and things that we surround ourselves with, then spending some time ensuring those are meaningful and valued is certainly worthwhile.

What talents do you have now or wish that you had? What do I wish that I learned as a child (maybe how to ski or how to play a musical instrument)? It may feel like it's too late in life to try those things; however, it's never too late, and you only have one life to live. If time and money were not barriers, what would you do? Are you spending your time doing things that make your heart happy?

Take a moment to assess your natural talents. Make a list of personal strengths and weaknesses. Are you using these strengths on a regular occurrence? Do the weakness areas present an opportunity to do better with some intentional effort, or are we spending time trying to hide/avoid those traits? Find the moments that bring you joy and repeat those often. Count your blessings and build on those. I believe that we all have strengths, and we should spend our time sharing them with the world.

> *"Focus on your strengths, not your weaknesses. Focus on your character, not your reputation. Focus on your blessings, not your misfortunes." — Roy T. Bennett, The Light in the Heart*

Those are the things where we should invest our time and ensure that we are pursuing talents that make our heart happy.

The Make-Up of a Successful Team

Growing up in a very sports-oriented family, I can't help but revisit the correlation and ponder the relationship between a great coach, quarter-back (leaders) and the players who make-up a winning team. How do these positions work together to create a successful team? Can teams succeed if they are missing any of these key elements? Probably not.

The Team (Employees)

We draft top talent (hire the best), and we get rid of those who don't make the cut (healthy turnover). This is true whether talking about football or companies. Can a football team compete if there are gaps in the defense, kicking team or special teams? Nope, and neither can your organization. You need people with different skills to make up your special teams and your departments, including sales, service, marketing, accounting and beyond.

Assess your team roster for gaps that need to be filled (create a strategic hiring plan). Ensure your best talent carries the ball (handles your most important work) and consider what happens if/when you have injuries (departures) or teammates who transition gracefully into retirement (succession planning).

Each team creates its own unique culture: putting in long hours of practice (work/overtime), developing personal relationships, attending events together, caring about the well-being of their teammates and creating an overall environment of trust, respect and teamwork.

It's important to ensure your team is bonding at an optimal level. Sometimes we have to facilitate these types of events, and we must be intentional regarding team engagement efforts (ask for feedback, survey or hold focus groups).

Your team plays an integral role in making the magic of your organization; ensure you have the right players working toward common goals.

Quarterback and Offensive Line (Key Leadership)

Imagine your key leaders as the quarterback and offensive line. These leaders work together to move the ball forward (create success in the organization). They hold huddles to communicate, provide encouragement and focus on the task at hand. And they develop respect and trust with the team and each other.

When the QB calls a play, the offensive line does whatever is necessary to make that play happen. Whether it's blocking, tackling, running, catching or creating gaps, in order to see success, everyone must do their part and do it well. Is your current QB and offensive line moving the ball down the field as desired (working toward that common goal and moving in the same direction)? Or is your team not able to get the fourth down (unable to move forward and growing stagnant)?

The Coach (A Business Culture-Shaping Coach)

Whether on a football team or within an organization, a strong coach is essential to developing the strategic plan and communicating that plan in an effective manner. The coach divides his/her time as a leader, mentor, motivator, strategic planner, cheerleader and more throughout the game.

He/she utilizes a playbook (strategic plan and tool kit) that is built over time, supplemented by years of experience and filled with ideas to drive success. The QB/offensive line (leaders) and team (employees) rely on the years of experience and preparation that the coach has to offer and listen because they know if they apply their muscle to the coach's wisdom, then great things will happen as they work together and navigate toward success. They execute on the plan and ensure everyone is working together.

Just as teammates change over time, so can the coach. Whether it's because of an antiquated approach (organizations must compete in today's competitive market) or the desire for a different plan coming from the GM (the board of directors), sometimes a new coach is needed.

If the game isn't headed in the direction you desire, then you must change up your teammates and/or find another coach to add to the bench strength of your team. New skills and perspective can be refreshing and needed. After all, we've seen the sidelines bursting with a support team (coaches, assistants, trainers, doctors, agents, referees, media, cheerleaders, mascots and more!). While you likely don't need a new mascot, it's critical to your organization to have the right people in place.

What's Next?

Having the right teammates on your bus and leading your team should resonate with you. After all, it's our people who are the core of our business. Stop and ask yourself some important questions: is it time to kick a few people off the bus? Is the bus running on fumes? What changes need to be made in order to ensure collaboration, build trust, streamline processes and represent your vision and values?

Take time to think about and strategically plan for talent within your organization. Utilize the THRIVE™ Model to game plan where you need to spend more time in order to level-up and build off the foundation. Alignment of talent and processes is imperative for a strong culture and organizational success.

> *"Great things in business are never done by one person. They are done by a team of people." – Steve Jobs*

Reflection Page: Talent Matters

What should we START doing to ensure our Talent Matters?

What should we STOP doing related to our Talent?

What should we CONTINUE doing related to our Talent?

Other Important Notes:

5

HEALTH (OF THE BUSINESS) MATTERS

THRIVE™ Model usage: Health (of the Business) Matters

Start at the foundation/roots:

- *Handbook/Required Postings and Training*: Starting off by taking a look at compliance-based projects, including the employee handbook, required trainings and required postings at your workplace and recommended for your specific industry.

- *Job Descriptions:* Reviewing job descriptions to ensure basic legal elements are met and that people understand their roles.

- *I-9 Process Created*: Committing to ensuring your I-9 process is adhered to and streamlined. Make sure it's built into your onboarding process and happens every single time. All of those things are forming a baseline of your compliance foundation.

- *Emergency Contact Form*: Implementing an Emergency Contact Form for all teammates, which includes important health information (such as a peanut allergy and where to access the

EpiPen) and multiple contacts to reach in case of an emergency event.

- *Diversity Awareness/Training*: Beginning the process of creating understanding and educating your team on Diversity Equity and Inclusion. At a minimum, organizations should train all teammates on why diverse perspectives matter and how to avoid discriminatory behaviors.

- *Employee Assistance Program (EAP)*: Ensuring that our team has support through a program that helps with personal problems and/or work-related issues, through assessments, counselling, referrals and follow-up services. These support programs are very important as they impact job performance, health, and mental/emotional well-being of our teammates.

Once you have this foundation, you can move upwards into the growth opportunities/branches:

- *Culture Deck*: Moving beyond the handbook. Many companies create something called a Culture Deck that demonstrates the pride in their organizational culture, the habits that make their team proud and the personal elements that make the organization standout from others. It shows outsiders the meaning of their work and gives a sense of how it feels to work at the organization while bringing organizational values to life.

- *Atmosphere & Workspace:* Recognizing another piece that makes organizations healthy is the ergonomics and environment in which we work. We want to make sure we have updated equipment that makes our employees feel good, allows them to work at peak productivity and doesn't cause them physical issues like neck strain or eyestrain. Our environment should reflect our brand but also keep our team engaged and comfortable. A positive work environment improves job satisfaction and overall performance. Always consider the culture that you wish to foster and create the kind of space that promotes aligned behaviors. Elements of nature can foster creativity and calmness. Bean bags and white boards give teams a space to brainstorm and get creative. Our work environment conveys a message about what we value, who we are and where we are going. There are design firms and office furniture companies that specialize in productive work environments. (Cindy Rubal at Herman Miller – I'm thinking of you here!)

- *Developmental Training:* Leveling up beyond required training and into developmental training options. Ask your team what types of things they would like to learn. We should work to enhance teammates' professionally (like learning how to use that new app/software) and personally with development of soft skills (time management or the art of listening to others).

- *Engaged in Personal Life:* Engaging in our team's personal life takes emergency contact forms to a whole new level. Understandably, we have to use care not to blend this knowledge with employment decisions. But we should know enough about teammates that we'd feel comfortable calling a spouse/partner if something happens at work or if we wanted to check-in to see how they are doing after a big surgery. I wouldn't have thought twice about administering that EpiPen if/when my teammate needed it; she had already showed me where she stored it in her desk and purse, and we had a practice device that we used to know how hard it had to be jammed into her leg to ensure it was effective. She wasn't going to die on my watch! I was ready. At the time, I didn't think much of it; I just cared about her as a person. She meant so much more than having an emergency form filed in my office. That type of genuine caring goes a long way with teammates.

- *Inclusive Community:* Observing and recognizing diverse perspectives (starting with diversity, equity and inclusion initiatives and training), moving beyond just the checklist mentality and truly embracing DE&I. As we have already discussed, this is critically important in order to create a balanced, forward thinking and respectful work culture. We have to do more than just cite its importance; we need to build a robust commitment to DE&I. I have some brilliant colleagues who have built a program around this complete with learning communities and so much more than checking off the compliance box. We must think creatively about how to apply DE&I across our organizations. We must ensure that we are attracting and retaining talent that comes from different walks of life (race, ethnicity, religion, gender, education and any other diversity element) so that we can obtain diverse perspectives and learn from views that are different from our own.

- *Holistic Wellness Plan:* Understanding and embracing wellness initiatives and the impact mental health has on your team (at work and home). Coming to the forefront in recent years (and especially prevalent due to societal stress/chaos like a pandemic) is the importance of mental health and how it impacts our teams both inside and outside of work. We cannot ignore the importance of addressing mental health concerns as a means of showing empathy and helping our team overcome hurdles. If we value our team's personal stability and happiness, we must try to help where we can with these issues. I am not a mental health professional, but I know enough to recognize the tender situation that exists surrounding this. Leaders should monitor mental health concerns with empathy and confidentiality, seek help where needed, train managers to see signs and partner with a good Employee Assistance Program (EAP). When your team's mental health is in a good place, teammates will be more productive contributors at work, home and society overall.

When we do these things, we ensure that the *HEALTH* of our business matters. We are building a foundation, making important choices, working our plan, engaging in strong habits and moving toward becoming a great place to work. When people matter, cultures THRIVE™.

Is your organization healthy enough to withstand turbulent times? Organizations need to build a strong foundation with legal and compliance guidelines and then grow from there. One of our biggest projects for clients often includes policy creation and handbook development. Does your organization have a legally approved handbook? Are you performing required training? Those are great places to start.

The overall health of a business will fluctuate; thus, a written plan will help keep you on track. Using the THRIVE™ Model to guide your legal/compliance needs is a good way to stay on course.

It's important to note, starting at the beginning of the THRIVE™ Model isn't required. As organizations assess their needs within the THRIVE™ Model heat map, we often advise organizations to start with "H" (Health of the Business) due to its critical legal importance. A compliance review ensures a strong foundation across the board. If gaps or blind spots come into view, you can address those as they arise. Build your checklists, update your handbook, ensure forms are updated, display required posters appropriately and schedule required training. Continue to look for new ways to do things and as always, get help when you need it.

Some organizations are so excited to do great things that they forget to build the foundation first. Think about your people processes one at a time. For example, hiring. Does your organization have a legal application? Are you using interview guides to ensure consistent and legal questions are being asked regardless of who is interviewing? Have you updated your handbook annually with new laws/regulations? If your current office manager (or COO) is handling these things, and she/he is not certified in human resources, please consider getting a consultant or coach to help guide the organization through these landmines. Setting the right path early will bring peace of mind, but it also reduces the headache of audits and financial pain related to costly Department of Labor (DOL) or Internal Revenue Service (IRS) fines.

Building a strong foundation with legal/compliance elements will mitigate risk, improve communication, lower stress levels and allow leadership to focus on growing the core business. Think of the health of your business today to ensure a foundation that sets the stage for organizational success tomorrow and beyond.

Another important piece in bridging any compliance gaps, includes scheduling a reoccurring (annual is ideal) legal review/audit. Once you have an initial handbook created, then you just need to update on a regular occurrence. National and state laws are continually changing and keeping up with all the changes can be an overwhelming task. Find a knowledgeable partner who can help you with this, whether your legal counsel or a compliance-minded HR person.

Occasionally, we hear organizations that don't believe they need a basic plan for legal and compliance needs. Even if you created a handbook five years ago, it's not sufficient to create it and forget it. We must be diligent to maintain and keep things updated. Just because your organization has been around the block a few times, doesn't mean it could never get tossed off track.

Case in point: thank you Matt Lauer[7]. Not for your inappropriate behavior but for reminding us that issues still exist related to harassment in the workplace. With the resurfacing of attention on a very important topic, we realize it's more pervasive than Lauer, as it was sprinkled all over news headlines. It's been a delicately (and sometimes not so delicately) discussed topic at many dinner tables and conference room tables alike. Perhaps it even strikes a chord and relates to an experience in your own life.

Wikipedia defines #MeToo as "a movement that began to spread virally in October of 2017 as a hashtag on social media in an attempt to demonstrate the widespread prevalence of harassment and assault, especially in the workplace."

A perpetual light shines on this topic; therefore, we must take a moment to think about our own organizations and how we are fostering a safe and healthy work environment. Employers cannot simply turn a blind eye and hope for the best. If that's your strategy, please start checking managers offices for creepy buttons under their desks that lock employees inside the office. (It was reported that Matt Lauer had one of those. Really. That's not a good strategy.)

As is our focus with this book, we encourage you to plan for the health of your business. Plan for compliance. Lay the foundation. Be intentional.

Here are a few important areas to focus on in order to get your organization on track towards a compliant and healthy culture: training, respect and leadership. Let's look at these a little more in depth.

> *"Train people well enough so they can leave. Treat them well enough so they don't want to." – Sir Richard Branson*

Training Is Key

As a baseline, there is required training that needs to take place. For example, sexual harassment training often comes across as a "check off" item for compliance. However, it needs to be handled on a deeper level. If your training is non-existent or is a quick one-hour lesson, employees will not have the ability to digest all of the layers of sexual harassment. Make sure employees understand how their behavior contributes to a positive work environment. Ensure that mutual respect is a requirement of ongoing employment with your organization. Go beyond the primary layer of sexual harassment training and ensure it reaches the depth of required respectful behavior.

One way to do this is to ensure that your handbook is updated annually (it's often a first line of defense), state that your organization does not support any form of harassment and outline what employees should do if/when they experience it. Additionally, you will want to update your non-retaliation stance and educate/train on that too. Ensure that leaders not only walk the talk as role models of good behavior, but also properly handle complaints in a timely fashion. Train them to handle it correctly, which is critical not only for addressing issues, but also for building trust.

Beyond required training, we also need to consider developmental training for our teams. This includes areas where the team desires additional improvement (worked into their performance goals) and where we see gaps in skills across the organization. During performance discussions, ask teammates what additional skills/knowledge they would like to obtain. Give them some latitude for personal and professional development, include some cross-training for business coverage of other departments. Loyalty and job satisfaction tend to increase when employees believe the organization is investing in them.

Who is the right party to train your team? A seasoned teammate might be the right person if he/she has subject matter expertise and respect of the team. For other legal matters, a good trainer is often your attorney (many will do this free of charge). It's also a good idea to find experts in the area of interest and allow them to impart their knowledge on your team. Partner with an outside consultant, coach or organization to garner subject matter expertise, to allow third party neutrality when needed (as they start to build a relationship for employees to voice concerns) and to learn from experts in their field.

Regardless of who conducts the training, be sure teammates are listening and learning throughout the training process. In order to apply to as many learning styles as possible, it's important to offer alternative vehicles for training (such as onsite/offsite, webinar or Zoom) and also offer different timeframes (90 minutes, lunch and learn, half day or full day).

As training commences, pay attention and assess as you go. What concerns are coming forward? What critical areas are being missed and need to be addressed? Where can you provide additional coaching or training to help fill in the gaps? Employers that strive to get better in this area should be applauded. Your team will appreciate your efforts.

> *"The growth and development of people is the highest calling of leadership." – Harvey S. Firestone*

Lead with Respect

Respect is free. I like to remind leaders to start with a foundation of respect. If only common sense was also common. Unfortunately, at many workplaces the little things add up quickly. And often times, those little things are negative and chipping away at your positive culture.

Perhaps you overheard an off-handed joke the other week about "going to the strip club." You may have laughed it off or just ignored it. Maybe a sexist undertone was present in discussion of health benefits (such as, "why are we employing all these women who are of child-bearing age?") Or maybe a certain job is only held by females at your organization and men "don't like that kind of work." While not always strikingly apparent, these types of innuendos can create a culture that is exclusive, insensitive and at a risk for becoming unsafe for all employees.

Establishing open discussions around these topics can assist in changing the entire tone of your organization. Avoid letting multiple, small poor practices lead to larger, dangerous practices. Death by a thousand paper-cuts. Strong leaders must address dysfunctional behaviors quickly. Nip them in the bud and keep moving forward; this will build respect and trust among your team.

Additionally, the behaviors that you repeat at your workplace will create the keys to success that build your culture. What positive behaviors exist within your workplace? Have you defined these behaviors to ensure everyone is on the same page? Have you tied those behaviors to habits that are naturally occurring within your organization?

In many organizations, there are positive intentions behind creating a strong culture, but not everyone has the same definition and interpretation. This is why defining behaviors is critical. Your team needs to understand the essential actions that guide their daily behaviors, and truly understand what's expected of them – now that's creating a culture worth celebrating. When people matter, companies thrive.

> *"I speak to everyone in the same way, whether he is the garbage man or the president of a university." – Albert Einstein*

Leaders Are Your Champions

Leaders set the tone. Good, bad, indifferent or inspiring. What tone are your leaders setting? Are they being role models of the desired behavior? Employees will naturally look up to leaders for guidance, answers, trust and often mirror leadership attitude and behaviors at work. It is vital for this group to set the tone that sexual harassment is not and will not be tolerated. Model the behavior we want to see of all teammates.

Actions speak louder than words. Own it. Follow the "Say/Do Ratio" (is what we are saying matching up with what we are doing or our behaviors?). If your leadership team cites policy but thinks they are above following the policy themselves, this is a recipe for disaster. Recognize that your teammates are watching leaders' behavior and modeling their behavior after what they witness. Accountability for leaders is essential – they are the champions of your brand. Make sure you have the right ones on board.

Leaders across America are in a unique place, moreover a very delicate one. We must continue to educate our teams, drive cultures of respect and always lead by example. Even when others in leadership roles are not living up to their title or position, and we cannot merely emulate their behaviors. We must do what we know is right and carry on in the best way we know how. Lead with respect. Hold other's feelings and heart with grace. Do what is right.

When Empathy and Ethics Collide

Empathy is the natural ability to understand the emotions and feeling of others. With this understanding, we can define narcissism as a deficit of empathy (lack of focus/caring about others, sense of entitlement, disregard for others and self-centeredness).

Shouldn't we all strive to be more empathetic? How does empathy benefit us? The answer is supported by science[9] – high levels of empathy are associated with *life satisfaction, rich social networks*, *healthy relationships*, *heightened workplace performance* and greater over-all *wellbeing*. Empathy paves the way for the common good.

But is there a direct link between empathy and ethics? And how does this impact our work culture?

I have always considered myself an empathetic person. My husband says I'm too trusting. As an entrepreneur, I have been faced with a continual pull-in by others who want to connect, network, learn and tap into my knowledge and expertise. I have always approached this with a "Givers Gain®" mentality (the more you give, the more you get in return – thanks to my BNI[8] networking group for these words of wisdom). I truly desire to help out of the goodness of my heart.

As I built my consulting business, I encountered a colleague that picked my brain and then started to claim these ideas, services, and even specific wording as her own. I understand that culture is a buzz word that many leaders are pushing in their organization, but not everyone approaches developing the culture in the same way. When I talk about culture, I am quick to recognize and thank the leaders who have imparted their knowledge on me (as you can see, it's all over this book). I also look for my own unique way to bring things forward and customize my approach as much as possible.

While a business relationship was forming and an agreement to share leads/clients was underway, we failed to ink an agreement beyond a verbal commitment. And sadly, she took full advantage of that. Just to make sure I wasn't making false assumptions, I followed up a few times. However, she disappeared without the courtesy of a returned phone call or email. My desire to share and teach was strong, but so were her lack of ethics. Therefore, she walked away with too much of the knowledge and expertise that I worked hard to earn.

While this experience was enlightening, it was also a sad moment where I realized (again) that I am too trusting and should not always assume the best in others. Empathy has a place in business, but we must remember that not everyone comes to the table with ethics that mirror your own. Ethics and integrity are intrinsic values, and it's difficult to teach to someone who is unwilling to learn.

Today I'm a bit more guarded, keeping my cards a little closer to the chest. And, yet, I refuse to let a negative situation like this guide my thoughts of others and overall interactions. I choose to set a higher bar. I choose to keep sharing, teaching and practicing empathy for others. I choose to find better partners and deliver a better service/product – all to build a more resilient business.

With all this in mind, here's the silver lining: *I* am the product that my clients often want to buy. My ethics, style, knowledge, empathy for others, personality and [insert whatever positive comment you would like here] are the reason that my clients engage and are very loyal. I cannot be replicated. The way that *I do* business cannot be stolen.

Even in a world where chaos ensues, we must carry on in the most ethical way we can – and remember that *you* cannot be replicated. Build a work culture where empathy is shown to others. Lead with the heart. And always let your ethical light shine. These things are invaluable as you create a healthy and compliant business where others can thrive.

As you may have guessed by now, this book is not a culture book about heritage, ethnicity, religion, background, race, etc. I will save that for experts in those areas. I abide by the golden rule: treating others as I wanted to be treated. And, as my dad taught me, value friends from all walks of life.

> *"I've got friends of all types." – David V. Rains*

While one might state the obvious (diversity is important in building a great workplace culture too!), this book covers a different type of culture. The culture we are creating is about an engaging workplace culture, built upon values, strengthened by our strong habits/processes (typically driven by human resource/heart rooted leaders and decision makers), in order to create a best place to work environment that thrives even when leaders are not looking. All of which includes diversity, equity and inclusion (DE&I).

DE&I has always been important – but make no mistake – the happenings related to social upheaval, the death of George Floyd, the Black Lives Matter movement and other sensitive situations in recent years have forced the hand of leaders to recognize the changes that must happen to move forward stronger and together. These issues cannot be ignored.

I recently had a prospective client decide that he didn't want to work with me because I "brought up DE&I" during an initial discussion about his HR needs. I was given this feedback from our mutual colleague who had recommended our connection. Apparently, he just wants "to do the work", get a scalable HRIS system to help him with business growth, and not really think about people concerns. Somehow it was conveyed that *I offended him. (*I'm getting kind of heated just thinking of this situation). I took a moment to compose my thoughts and responded to the colleague that I was thankful for his feedback (trying to be gracious here). However, I ensured to add that it was good that we didn't wind up working together, as this is not the kind of short-sited client that I want to represent. I'm glad he showed his true colors early, and I didn't have to waste time trying to help this tiger change his stripes.

Part of a healthy business is celebrating the diversity within it. DE&I is just good business. Good for all involved and good for a strong workplace culture. Respecting others who are different from us (guess what, everyone is different from us) and valuing diverse perspectives is the baseline. Then we start to address bigger issues like diversity recruitment and saving space for minority leaders so they get a chance to participate at all levels. And from here, we build up.

. . .

Mental Health Matters

We had almost 2,500 employees. Only one of them believed she was a chicken. I tell this story because it's a clear case for mental health struggles, but also because we can learn from these situations, and they increase our empathy for others. And while we did go down the path of getting Chicken Lady mental health help, the lessons we learned along the way still make me smile even today.

"Katie" was struggling. We first came to know this when stabbed herself on the call-center floor with a metal letter opener. Now, this situation was before my time with the HR team, so I wasn't around for the scary and messy scene that unfolded. However, I heard stories of its existence like a really bad reality show. Blood all over the place. People passing out. Ambulances. Rumors spreading that someone had been stabbed upstairs. By who? Did we have a crazy mass murderer taking over the building? People were afraid, and it took some time to settle the masses. The ending story sounded more like a game of Clue; it was Katie with a letter opener in the library. We don't know exactly why she did this – maybe for attention or maybe to give some physical pain to rival the emotional pain she was experiencing. Again, we don't really know. But it was definitely the first story I ever heard about Katie.

Katie also had what we will call...chicken tendencies. What I mean is that Katie thought she was a chicken. Katie was a big fan of chickens. She had a bunch at home as her pets. She loved them very much - just like many of us who have four-legged fur babies. These were her two-legged feather babies. However, they were more than just pets – they were her family.

Katie loved them so much that she wanted to be like them. She would cluck, scratch her feet, flap her arms and cock her head back and forth. It wasn't normal human behavior - it scared coworkers. Some saw it as harmless, but others were really scared. Many requested seats that were not near her. And of course, the letter opener situation didn't help matters.

We tried to understand Katie and have empathy for her unusual chicken infatuation. We worked with her doctor in an attempt to minimize the ongoing disruptions at work. When the doctor requested that she get a service dog to help her adjust to a more "normal" support animal, we were excited to see if that might help. Soon after the doctor's request, I was thrilled to hear that Katie brought Rover to work on a leash. And everyone was pretty excited to meet Rover...until we weren't.

You see, Rover was a stuffed animal. Katie didn't take the doctor's request seriously because she had a house full of chickens (not something a dog would be a good fit for), so in her mind, she did the next best thing. Katie got a stuffed animal. She was literally dragging a stuffed animal all over the call center. Barking for him. Wagging his tail. Picking up his poo. Growling at coworkers that he felt were bad people. Her teammates were less than thrilled, and their patience was running out. Oh my – this wasn't turning out how we had hoped.

We tried to be understanding of Katie's new pet and the spiraling situation among the team, as we knew she was struggling. We wanted to be part of the solution. We required Katie to attend counselling through our EAP services and asked for her doctor's recommendation.

One rainy day, an employee came running into the HR department yelling, "There's a chicken in a cage under a car in the parking lot! And it's going to drown if we don't do something quickly!" Another employee came in behind her yelling, "I'm calling the SPCA!" (Do they handle chickens, too?!) Our HR team looked around in disbelief. I knew whose chicken this was, so I jumped out of my seat to go find Katie.

When I asked Katie about the poor chicken in the parking lot she said, "Well, we have a vet appointment and she couldn't very well sit in the car all day. Plus, it was nice out this morning." I agreed, she could not sit in the car all day. But she couldn't sit under the car in the rushing water to potentially drown in the rain either. The change in weather meant we needed to figure out another plan. We allowed Katie to leave, save her chicken, attend the vet appointment and agreed to call her later.

Unfortunately, this type of interruption was all too common. And we were spending a lot of time addressing Katie's special pet needs. Our leadership teams' patience was wearing thin, never mind that we had a business to run. The main issue was due to the continuing interruptions at work. I felt pulled between compassion and empathy for Kate's fragile mental health and terminating her employment as I was instructed to do.

The idea surfaced to continue to support her counselling with the Employee Assistance Program (EAP), which at this point we'd already tried it a few times. We hoped to continue to address her mental health issues in a sensitive way with the guidance of a counsellor. The new idea was to create a departure plan and severance agreement to allow her to transition out, to help her financially and also to encourage her to move on and find employment success elsewhere.

We offered Katie $6,000 ($1,000 for every year of service), which was a lot of money for someone making $10.00 per hour. It was not commonplace to give severance to hourly employees when we parted ways with them, but it certainly felt like the right thing to do. And this situation was anything but common.

I guess we hoped Katie would be excited at the large amount, quickly accept it, sign off and move on to another fine institution. One with better chicken support systems than we were able to provide. I prepped the severance letter and gave Katie a call (my colleague Cheryl joined as a witness to our discussion).

When she picked up the phone, there was a lot of clucking and commotion in the background. I could barely hear her, but she said she could hear me just fine. Our conversation was respectful and rather short and sweet as I reviewed the details of the letter and encouraged her to talk to an attorney to ensure the letter was acceptable. Her only sticking point: she couldn't possibly accept "the devil's number" (six) as part of her $6,000 amount. I asked if she'd accept one penny less: $5,999.99, and she quickly agreed to the idea. I hoped Katie would never turn that check over and see all those nines as inverted sixes!

The next step was to wait the required revocation period, and then we'd provide a payment in a lump sum. As we tried to wrap up the call, Katie broke into a wondrously loud chorus of the song "Wooly Bully" by Sam The Sham and the Pharaohs (lyrics: "*Matty told Hattie, about a thing she saw, had two big horns, and a wooly jaw, Wooly bully, Wooly bully"*). As I ponder this 10 years later, I cannot help but wonder if the song has any meaning? Google suggests the song is a "conversation between Matty and Hattie about a thing they saw, and the desirability of developing dancing skills, although no attempt is made to synthesize these divergent topics," which doesn't seem to apply here. To me, the word "bully" stands out. Maybe Katie was feeling bullied and this was how it came out. But, alas, I will never know.

Katie sang the same Wooly Bully chorus over and over. We listened and waited. And waited. After about 15 minutes, she was still singing. Cheryl and I weren't exactly sure what to do. Our company had a zero-tolerance policy for hanging up on a customer. Katie knew this policy well after six years in the call center, and we believed that she was testing us to see how we would handle a challenging "customer" call. Or maybe, we could have chalked it up to her continued break from reality and ongoing mental issues. I wasn't sure, but I wanted to remain respectful and empathetic. Cheryl and I pressed mute and discussed our options. All the while, Wooly Bully continued.

Ultimately, we created a game plan and executed. I stated, "Katie, thank you so much for our discussion today. Please call me or Cheryl if you have any questions. We really do wish you well." And with that, we hung up. Cheryl and I looked at each other for a moment in disbelief. Wow. That was a new one. We were not sure if/when we would hear from Katie again. I marked my calendar to follow up with a check-in call after the revocation period, just in case I didn't hear back from her.

The next day we received a call from our store in the Tri-County area. It was a joint call from their HR representative and the head of their security department. They explained that there was a woman in front of the store who was marching back and forth, carrying a sign and asking customers to boycott with her. I asked how they knew that she was one of our employees? Apparently, when they approached the woman to see how they could help her, she explained that she used to work at the call center and was happy to be let go because we do not treat chickens respectfully enough. Her sign stated it all: "Chicken Haters."

Ahhh, Katie. It wasn't really the chickens we were trying to help and support. It was the person impacted by the chickens. And we make every effort to handle it as respectfully as we could. We were patient as we confidentially worked through issues and disturbances. We made referrals to the EAP and worked with the doctor to meet his requests. We followed up with personalized coaching. We had absolutely no ill will toward chickens.

Oh, yes, I forgot to mention this important detail: Katie was marching back and forth that nice fall day in a full-on chicken suit – this was her big, final performance (thank goodness it wasn't summer, or I would have been even more worried about her passing out in the hot and restrictive chicken mask).

We didn't take any action that day. We didn't ask her to leave. Instead, we let her grow naturally tired of the boycott and eventually she went home.

The next week, I received her signed severance letter in the mail. She was ready to move on. I ensured the severance compensation processed appropriately, and we never heard from Katie after that.

The joy of employee relations.

What can we learn from this story? Compassion. Everyone has their own personal issues. We don't know all the details and challenges going on in their life. Where possible, we must try practice some level of empathy. Think of ways we can support people during their darkest hours. This was a hard one – I'm sure there are elements that I could have handled better, but I'm confident that I never lost patience and never disrespected Katie during a challenging situation. Cheryl and I worked really hard to make this as good of an outcome as possible for Katie and the company.

Albeit a funny story later, I still fondly think of sweet clucking Katie every time I walk into that department store. Maybe we can all learn a new level of walking in another person's shoes when we think of Katie, and we should remember the importance of addressing mental health concerns – always with compassion and respect.

Carry on, sweet girl. I hope you are well.

Learning about Diverse Perspectives

"Pat" was known to be a bully. And in our call center environment, we were all too familiar with the cry of "she stole my chair" as employees sought to assert their claim to office space and equipment in a building that operated around the clock. It was a big deal to swap chairs with one that rolled better, leaned back sufficiently and/or adjusted correctly – as I guess many chairs were in poor working order. The chair battles were a real thing (I wish we could have just purchased new ones, but our corporate budgets did not allow for that).

When Pat came down to HR, I could tell she was angry. I ushered her into a private interview room to see what was going on. My colleague, "Natasha," joined as a witness (another situation where we knew it was necessary due to Pam's irate behavior and history of aggression).

There was another argument on the floor about chairs – whose chair belonged to whom. It was another case of "stealing" on third shift again. One of Pat's coworkers had placed some black duct tape on the arm rest of her chair, and, therefore, she knew the chair in question belonged to her, yet somehow it kept showing up at Pat's desk. The story just kept going in circles.

I was trying hard to listen and stay interested, but I was growing tired of the great chair debate. At this point, Pat was angrily ranting over and over some version of the same story: "I told Julie you got the wrong one." I suggested that maybe Julie didn't know she had the wrong chair, and that it was not something we should get so angry about. Pat just kept repeating the same phrase, "I told her she had the wrong one!" I could not make sense of this – why was she so angry about a chair? Grab another one and move on.

Natasha asked Pat to excuse us for a moment and we stepped outside and into our boss' office. Natasha has giggling as she said, "Um, Melanie...girl, we need to get you hip to Pat's language. These are fighting words in Pat's view. She's saying: 'You got the wrong one" – as in you messed with the *wrong person* and not the wrong chair." She bobbed her head with sassiness and attitude as she said it.

Just hearing Natasha say it made more sense. Fighting words? Geeze - was I ignorant to what was going on here. I was trying to make sense of a discussion in which I didn't know my audience well enough. I was trying to fit this situation into my own perspective. Natasha was coaching me on the nuances of listening to tone and inflection, but also knowing my audience better. It's important that we recognize and respect that we all have different backgrounds and perspectives that we bring to the table. I was naïve to think this argument was only about a chair.

My HR colleagues got quite a kick out of this situation, and they often would jest: "You got the wrong one today, Melanie?" Yep, I had the wrong one. The wrong understanding. It was a good opportunity for personal growth. I'd work harder to know my audience better, expand my horizons in valuing others' perspectives and listen closer in the future.

***Personal Application*: Health (of the Business) Matters**

Just as we apply the THRIVE™ Model to our business, we can apply these areas to our personal life as well. How does health show up regularly in our personal life? It's important to think about health in a variety of ways, including our mental, emotional, intellectual and physical nature.

Take a moment to stop and assess how you currently feel about your personal health situation. Do you get enough sleep at night? Do you have a high-stress job? Do you find yourself snapping at your kids all too often? Are you drinking plenty of water throughout the day? Are you in a sedentary job, and, if so, are you able to offset that with walks and exercise?

Health is not something that we should only focus on during our annual New Year's resolution making. It's something that we must continually work to improve and develop positive habits. Of course, I know this is easier said than done. And for the purpose of this book – I will try not to place too much "weight" on the matter (that's a funny play on words).

At some point in my youth, I think around junior high - I recall a discussion with my dad where he suggested that I needed to lose weight or kids might not want to be my friend (because as we all know kids can be mean, and those awkward junior high years are often the worst).

And my reply was this: "But, dad, you're fat, and you have all kinds of friends!"

This makes me laugh – as apparently, I was wise beyond my years. This is no surprise to those who know me, but I've struggled with weight my entire life. There wasn't a time in my life when I wasn't chubby. I've tried every diet (and eating healthy), exercised regularly throughout the years including playing all kinds of sports, walking the neighborhood day-in-and day-out, tested hormones, checked thyroid levels, running the medical gauntlet (it was discovered that I have Celiac Disease – but somehow in my family that does not make us deathly ill and thin, but rather allows us to hold onto weight. Yay!).

There is no magic pill; I continually strive to do better. I'm happy knowing that I don't have any major health conditions, and for that I am thankful. Health matters, and that's my goal. And guess what – I still have plenty of friends. We must not let a number on the scale dictate our happiness. Get up and move, eat as well as you can and work to be a good person – it's more than just those numbers on a scale, but a healthy view of life.

As we know, health is about more than just our physical appearance and medical statistics. Emotionally, how are we relating to others?

> *"Relax" – David Rains (with accompanying hand gesture, signifying calm down* and slow down)

In the past when I heard this word, "Relax," I would have a visceral, negative reaction. A hair-raising on my neck, gut-punching, WTH, who has time to relax kind of reaction!? Needless to say, I don't relax well.

Like most working mothers of three, with two dogs (why in the world did I get that new puppy?), running my own business, supporting five networking groups, serving on two boards, coaching soccer, running kids to sports, clubs and dance, maintaining a house and two cars and more (you know the list, I probably don't have to spell it out, right?), I'm typically on the go and rarely find time to slow down.

Dad liked to say: "I run circles around 'em," which meant that others cannot keep up, and he doesn't slow down, or he gets things done.

However, running on fumes a million miles a minute is not the answer. There is joy in finding the brake and taking a moment to slow down. If nothing else, COVID taught us this, and we had no choice but to slow down as the world was forced to throw on the emergency brake. Lesson from a pandemic: you must slow down. Learn to relax. Noted. However, I'm not sure that's quite what I had in mind.

Creating the space that I needed to push the pause button and find my inner introvert has been invaluable. This included more reading, writing, napping (one of my favorite activities) and taking walks. And while I missed seeing people in person (I missed the hugs), I figured out what JOMO is (Joy of Missing Out). The calendar on the refrigerator wasn't packed with things to do (no sports, no dance, no birthday parties or concerts and no more shuttling the kids to practice). In the fall we started to see these things creeping back onto the calendar, but at a slower pace.

As we navigate the new normal and through challenging times, it will be critically important to determine which things are truly worth adding back to the calendar. Not all things are worth the return.

Difficult times will come and go. In an effort of self-improvement, we must ask ourselves: what positive elements can we take with us and what can we learn from? The world is forever changed. Now everyone knows how to Zoom and so we add that to our communication devices where appropriate (ex. I loved teacher conferences by Zoom!). My silver lining: whatever is thrown our way, we must learn to relax, take things in stride and slow down, just as dad always said.

No matter what your current personal situation, make a pledge to yourself to try to add a few healthy habits into your life. Take a moment to assess which habits are not serving you well and which ones build you up. Work to say no to things that drain your emotional tank. The power of "No" should not be ignored. Although it can be hard to muster the word, I have found it helpful to say something like this, "I appreciate the invite, but I cannot commit 100% of myself to that right now. But thank you for thinking of me!"

Try your new healthy habits for 30 days. Start small and let the snowball effect take hold. Doing something for 30 days will help you establish it as a habit. It's a great place to start and then keep making small improvements to be 1% better every day.

Reflection Page: Health (of the Business) Matters

What should we START doing to ensure the Health of Business

Matters?

What should we STOP doing related to our Health?

What should we CONTINUE doing related to our Health?

Other Important Notes:

6

RETENTION MATTERS

<u>THRIVE™ Model usage:</u> Retention Matters

Start at the foundation/roots and assess that your organization offers:

- *Basic Benefits:* Offering medical, prescription drug, dental, and vision coverage is often seen as a baseline for benefit coverage. Smaller organizations are not always able to offer these things, and if that's the case – offer a benefits summary with connections who can help employees obtain self-funded/ independent plans.

- *Competitive Wages:* Offering the most competitive wages you are able to within your industry is ideal. This is good for your team morale and should also help with retention.

- *Rewards and Recognition:* Motivating employees is important within an organization, and we must think of ways to do this beyond compensation. Instituting different forms of reward and building on respect for all teammates, we can show appreciation to the team by offering informal or formal praise in a timely manner for a job well done. This seems like a basic tenet of a good culture and although simple, it's often overlooked.

- *Team-Minded Atmosphere*: Ensuring that you are always not only thinking of your employees, but also allowing them to participate in some decision making, such as goal setting, employee surveys, all-town meetings and feedback opportunities. We place great importance on making sure the team feels valued.

- *Fun Events:* Planning events that the team will enjoy like picnics, happy hours and/or company parties both within and outside regular working hours. This should take into account a variety of interests with team input.

Once you have this foundation, you can move upward into the growth opportunities/branches and level up by offering:

- *Above and Beyond Benefit Plans:* Taking your current benefit offerings and ensuring that you have the lowest deductibles, highest coverage, widest network, and overall just the best plan possible offered for individuals and families. Thinking outside the box might include voluntary benefits or work perks that are outside the norm of offerings and mean something to your team (flexible workspace/time is often an overlooked but very important work perk). Other ideas may include tuition reimbursement or repayment, pet insurance, life insurance, dry cleaning, childcare or some of the other creative ideas discussed in this chapter.

- *Market-Leading Compensation:* Moving beyond just being competitive, your organization has opted to lead the market in regards to compensation. This may include additional comp strategies like incentive plans, bonus opportunities, stock options and/or other ways to supplement the base rate of pay.

- *Meaningful Appreciation:* Understanding the motivators behind meaningful appreciation versus just a pat on the back. Proper communication often lies at the center of accomplishing this in a meaningful way. Be specific and timely in the praise, and add a personal element that shows you care and are not just checking the appreciation off your list of things to do.

- *Owner-Minded Atmosphere:* Thinking about the team is important, but we want to ensure the organization is set up to succeed, too. Therefore, we watch for waste, try to save money and make decisions as if it was our own company.

- *Engagement Committee:* Having fun events is important, but getting the team involved in planning and participating in things that they really want to do will build overall engagement and camaraderie. It's also a good idea to form a committee so that multiple departments are represented, and different ideas are implemented. For example, when I worked at the design firm, our creative employees wanted to do things to feed their creative side like take walking tours of downtown to view the architecture, go blacksmithing or hold lunch and learns where we learned to brew beer or bind books. Always something new with that crew, and it was refreshing.

When we do these things, we ensure that *RETENTION within* our business matters. We are building a foundation, making important choices, working our plan and engaging in strong habits – on our way to becoming a great place to work and leaving a culture legacy that will make us proud. When people matter, cultures THRIVE™.

> *"Culture is the number one reason employees stay or leave your company." – Steve Browne, HR on Purpose*

Everyone wants to make more money – that's a basic human desire. However, people will not stay at your organization for money alone. Sadly, compensation is frequently cited as the reason employees leave (NOTE: we should also interpret this as "better opportunity," which is synonymous with "I'm going to make more money somewhere else").

It doesn't take a brain surgeon to realize, but money is cited most because it's the easiest scapegoat. As the employee is giving feedback during an exit interview (please make sure you offer one) or talking to a supervisor/HR as they depart, it's hard to tactfully tell someone it's because your culture or leadership is terrible. It's much easier to take the high road, avoid burning bridges and veer away from what might feel like a personal attack (after all, they are leaving you – poor shmuck – to work in the terrible culture). And, so, they stick with the "better opportunity" somewhere else shtick.

It's important to recognize that people are motivated differently, and incentives should be customized to the extent possible. Our findings demonstrate that most employees desire *rewards* (compensation, benefits, time-off, training and development opportunities) and *recognition* (appreciation for meaningful work and praise from respectful leaders). A blend of rewards and recognition are important factors that help organizations retain teammates and keep them happy for years to come.

I'll say it again: everyone wants to make more money. It's important that your wages are competitive enough to keep good people and not a continuing pain-point. Decide what your compensation approach will be (lead, lag or be steady with the market). I usually recommend that clients perform a compensation analysis every three years to ensure that compensation is on target within your industry and competitive in the market.

Over the past five years, I have surveyed 40+ organizations related to their employee engagement and culture. The trends that surface over and over are similar. Aside from pay, employees desire: 1. Better Communication 2. Better Benefits 3. Better Leadership. How is your organization focusing on and making improvement in these critically important areas? Let's take a moment to talk about each of these a little more.

Better Communication

No matter the size or industry, every organization needs improvement with communication. I've never heard of an organization that has communicated enough, and there are always gaps. All too often employees feel left out and that their input doesn't really matter. Simple solution: do an engagement survey (ideally with a neutral third party facilitating it).

What is serving your organization well and what needs a new approach? Our communication efforts are challenged on a regular basis with legal and regulatory updates, societal changes, generational differences, style and preference, technology knowledge and more. Employers cannot bury their heads in the sand to avoid change.

In fact, I believe that top-notch employers fight the *traditionalist* mindset – knowing that there is value in how things were done in the past, but exponential value in the ability to embrace new technology, ideas and tools to improve over time. Whether that's allowing antiquated polices or avoiding Zoom, we must be willing to try new things. Technology improvements are mainstream and improve efficiency, productivity and communication, which are critical components for our culture success. We must embrace new ways of communicating and getting things done.

A large part of communicating better is simply done by showing that you care and genuinely listening better. We have two ears and one mouth, and we should use them accordingly. You learn more when you listen than when you talk. Yet so often people are talking more, listening less and filling in the blank space with annoying vocal fillers. People talk over others. They are already thinking of their response before the other person is done talking. In order to improve communication, everyone must get comfortable with the quiet moments, listen generously and show that you really do care about what the other person is saying.

Another important element is considering the *methods* by which your organization is communicating. Are you communicating in a way that others can hear you? If your team prefers in-person messages and you send tons of emails, you are not using their preferred communication style. If your client prefers a text check-in, but you refuse to send text messages and leave a voice mail, is that effective communication? I recommend that organizations use multiple methods (email, text, meetings, calls, messaging, etc.) to cover all their bases. But most importantly, open up the discussion to customize your delivery method to the style desired by the receiving party where possible. That way we ensure that our message has the best chance of being heard.

Every organization has communication challenges. A great way to bridge the gap is through engagement surveys and also performing a self-assessment of your own communication skills. Let technology help where it can, be sensitive to the method and never underestimate the value of the human moment.

Better Benefits

Beyond compensation, another common complaint is about benefit plans and the issues surrounding them. When an organization is not happy with their benefit offering, often the benefit advisor is to blame (they have grown lax in their follow up and approach, with little/no fresh ideas to drive costs down).

Perform an annual assessment of your benefit advisor to ensure they are acting in your employee and organization's best interest. Blindly accepting rate increases is a sign of a lazy broker; they must do better. Find a benefits advisor that fights for your best interest and goes above and beyond to make good things happen for your organization. (Kathleen Crawford, Bailey & Company comes to mind. She sees the link to benefits and a strong culture and delivers on point customer service. If your advisor is lacking, look her up on LinkedIn. You will not regret it!)

When leaders take the time to review benefit offerings, there's a close link to ongoing culture success. Unfortunately, many employers get too comfortable with their benefit offerings and fail to think outside the box. What kinds of plans are you offering?

Start by thinking broadly: medical, dental and vision coverage. Yes, those are important. But are you offering other benefits or perks that are outside the box?

Additional supplemental benefits range from common to unique and may include: prescription coverage, STD/LTD, life insurance, EAP programs, pet insurance, free flu shots, biometric screenings and retirement plans/401(k), ideally with a match.

Benefits also extend into vacation time, PTO, paid PTO (giving bonuses for taking vacation time) and holidays (most organizations offer between 7 to 11 days; where does your organization fall in that range? Do you want to lead or lag in the market? Giving employees time off is a great way to show them that you care about their self-care and work/life balance. Employers should want their team to take time to recharge. Studies show that employees who take time off are more productive than those who do not.

Consider going beyond these offerings and offer unique options that may include: professional development through tuition reimbursement (current and new) and tuition repayment (for old school loans), wellness incentives (everyone gets a Fitbit, a gym membership or potentially harnessing the power of the nap pod), onsite coffee/snacks, relaxed dress code, lucrative referral programs, summer picnics, incentive plans and performance bonuses, engagement committees, personal and professional training, standing desks and ergonomic office equipment, off-site team building events or discounts on mobile phone service.

One important benefit not to be forgotten is training and development, which is an especially important benefit in today's workplace. Employees want more than just "climbing the corporate ladder;" instead, most are interested in a jungle gym with a variety of options for mobility. We cannot assume that every employee only wants upward movement, but we can empower them through growth with lateral moves, new challenges in their current role, different responsibilities and investment in their overall skills. Furthermore, we cannot and should not make every top performer a supervisor. Not everyone is cut out to lead others, they might just be really good at their craft, and that's ok. Build them up and ensure they are respected. Allow them to have guru status and let them teach others.

Training takes the form of both required training and developmental training, and employers need to offer both. Ask teammates what they wish to learn each year and work those into the training budget. When I worked with creatives within a design firm, the team wanted Adobe, a 3D printer and cross-functional training, which we made happen through a rotation and monthly "Lunch and Learns." Bonus: these were developed as a shared responsibility among the team as they took turns leading and teaching each session and were completely free to the company (we often packed lunches). If you elect to bring in an external trainer, remember that a group session can be held for a better price than individual training, so try that route in order to benefit the most employees.

Employers must make training and development a priority or your best teammates will leave. Plain and simple. While you may not be able to do all those things, I bet you can do a few. And it's important to note that doesn't mean all of these need to be 100% paid for by the company. I have many clients who offer these benefits as 100% employee contribution, and employees are thrilled to have them.

After we've thoroughly reviewed our rewards within the organization, now we must look at our internal recognition platforms. Meaningful work and feeling valued matters to today's workforce. How do we ensure people know they are appreciated and their work is valued? Two key areas demonstrate this – showing appreciation and better leadership. Let's dive into this a bit more.

Appreciation for Meaningful Work

Think about a time when you were shown appreciation for something that you did, whether it was in your personal life or at work. How did it make you feel?

While it can often be a very simple gesture, verbal praise is the easiest form of recognition and appreciation to give. Sadly, it might be the easy factor that gets praise all too often overlooked or forgotten!

In order to have the most impact when providing praise, you will want to be specific when you deliver it. For example, if you're praising an employee for a job well done, you do not want to just say, "Great job, Sally!" This is too vague and easily forgotten. Instead, you want to say something like. "Sally, thank you so much for doing a great job with that difficult customer today. I really liked how you took a challenging situation and worked diligently to resolve it for the client. Well done!" Sally knows you appreciated her work, what she did specifically and hopefully she will repeat that behavior down the road. And as we are learning about behaviors that drive culture, it's those repetitive behaviors which we deem as aligned with our values (Keys to Success) that are the foundation of our habits to foster culture.

Strive to recognize employees at a level that drives teamwork and recognizes collaboration, being careful about supporting too much internal competition. If creativity is something that you want to see employees demonstrating, then leaders must ensure to recognize creative and innovative ideas, not conformity and doing things the way they've always been done. Stop and take a moment to think about the actions that you truly want to see repeated. Then determine if you are supporting and recognizing those so that they are praised, positive feedback, and pushing for future repetition. Incentivizing the wrong thing will bring about the wrong results.

> *"You need to be aware of what others are doing, applaud their efforts, acknowledge their successes, and encourage them in their pursuits. When we all help one another, everybody wins." – Jim Stovall*

Praise in public, and criticize in private. I'm certain that my parents taught me this long ago, but it's also very important in the business setting when coaching employees. We must avoid putting others in embarrassing moments that their pride cannot easily recover from. If an employee messes up, we should address it in a timely fashion.

That doesn't mean immediately and in front of others. instead, call the employee to your office or speak by phone (both preferred over an email but sometimes that might suffice). Ask if there is another way that the situation might have been handled (many times the employee already knows there was an issue) and come to a resolution together so that it doesn't happen again. Don't be sorry, be better. It's ok to make mistakes – we are all human – but we must learn from them.

Another area to remember is that not all people desire or appreciate *public* praise. Some would rather have private recognition with an email or hand-written note. Great leaders ensure their appreciation message is delivered in the way at the employee can best hear it. Otherwise, the reception is fuzzy, and it's not delivered with clarity. Its intended desire (excitement for the praise and continued positive behavior) falls woefully short, and we may not get the repeat behavior that we wanted.

Our desire is that teammates take in these moments of praise, and the positive comments improve performance and compound like the snowball effect. One moment of praise builds into another. Up, down and laterally. These moments of building each other up can be contagious if you let them! Now you just need to get it started with verbal affirmations and praise.

> *"Put some mustard on him" – David Rains*

(Dad's highest praise – used when someone does something really good, usually athletically – I can recall him saying this about my brother Greg quite often. It was positive motivation and praise, which we yearned to receive!)

Better Leadership

We have heard the saying that employees don't leave companies, they leave a bad manager. This is so often the case. While making more money is a basic human desire, people will not stay at your organization for money alone. In addition to the communication and benefits improvements we have already discussed, employees desire respect and trust from leadership, meaningful work and a positive work culture.

> "The quality of a leader is reflected in the standards they set for themselves." --*Ray Kroc, McDonald's*

If the road to nowhere is paved with excuses, then the road to turnover is paved with bad managers. Leaders set the tone for the culture of the organization. And while everyone has a hand in the culture, the example is set at the top, and it flows down from there. However, we must be mindful of the hierarchy fallacy. While many organizations operate with that top-down approach, it can become stifling and micro-managerial. This is not what people want.

True leadership comes from those who are willing to roll up their sleeves and get in the trenches with their team; they are not above doing the work themselves. They share in the pain and the success. They take more blame and less credit. Ask yourself: do I set the example that I hope others will follow? Or do I preach rather loudly and don't believe that the rules apply to me? Your team is watching closely – be sure to lead by example.

> "A good leader leads the people from above them. A great leader leads the people from within them." --*M.D. Arnold, Physician & Author*

It's human nature to want to do good work. No one shows up each day and thinks, "Wow, I hope that I can really stink this place up today." With that in mind, the best leaders can harness this desire and multiply it for the greater good of the organization. Find each person's strength and allow them to use that strength over and over for the good of the company (and pride for themselves).

Too often micro-managing styles exist in the workplace, which will not build the culture that we desire. There seems to be this sad waffling between over-managing and absentee management and a struggle to find a good balance in the middle. If we operate with the idea that things are managed and that people are lead and treated with respect, we can create a culture of thought leadership founded on communication that values speaking straight and with genuine candor.

My colleague Steve Van Valin with Culturology made me aware of the amazing work of Teresa Amabile and Steven Kramer who wrote *The Progress Principle*[10]. They explain (after a laborious analysis of nearly

12,000 diary entries provided by 238 employees in 7 companies) how managers can foster progress and enhance inner work life every day.

In fact, progress is the prime motivator for workplace happiness. Just like earning a Girl or Boy Scout badge or leveling up on your next video game, the power of progress is a strong one. In the workplace that means recognizing advancement of projects, tasks and the like.

Studies within *The Progress Principle* sought to prove this over and over. In one study they had leaders rank the top five motivators of work (incentives, recognition, interpersonal support, clear goals and progress). *The results revealed unawareness of the power of progress at every level of management.* When leaders work to harness this power, we see strategy execution due to great performance of teammates within the organization.

Every leaders' job description should include facilitating progress in team's work. Oh, and the key here is also that the work is meaningful. Check out Amabile's work for more details and stories about igniting joy, engagement and creativity through *progress* within your organization. You will not be disappointed in this gold mine of untapped potential (learn more on the reference page).

Reward and Recognition Result in Retention

Which came first, the chicken or the egg? Should we focus on retention or turnover? Recruit good people and treat them well. When our focus is on treating people well, then we will have less turnover.

Turnover is expensive and costs organizations insurmountable amounts of money each year. And not only does it result in a substantial loss of money, but also it leads to productivity issues, poor morale and a revolving door of expertise and knowledge within organizations. The question everyone is asking is, why does turnover happen?

Keeping your best talent is critically important, and companies spend a lot of money and time working to keep those people on the bus. But it's equally important (sometimes more so) that we help the organization by assisting toxic teammates off the bus. This addition by subtraction speaks volumes to the people who remain at the organization. When we show toxic teammates the door, it draws the line in the sand as to what will be tolerated and reinforces what's acceptable behavior and what's not.

While some will lean one direction and some the other – the answer varies per organization. However, there is a universal question we can all ask: what if we changed our perspective, and rather than wasting money due to turnover costs (think re-recruitment, re-training, re-on-boarding, etc.), we buckled down and focused on proactive prevention and made a serious investment in retention.

So why does all of this matter to your organization? Here are a few key actions that we see when employers invest in retention:

- Money is saved (think training, recruitment, on-boarding, etc.)
- Morale is boosted and employees are more engaged
- Absenteeism goes down
- Production improves (because engaged people do better work!)
- Communication gaps minimize as teams work together better
- Retention of employees becomes the norm (Adiós turnover problems!)
- Customer/client satisfaction goes through the roof
- Overall culture is enhanced, and referrals of other good employees increase
- Profits soar because of all the above

One of my favorite stories links the need for team appreciation and leadership's desire to show metrics and correlate that into showing overall value. While we can do this with turnover statistics and survey results, there is also strong intrinsic value placed on retention of great people that numbers just cannot rectify.

Show Me the Numbers

HR leaders are often people-centric. *And* we know that it's good to support our cause with metrics. Sometimes it can be hard to put a number on feelings, and yet when you are dealing with people, feelings matter. HR leaders strive to validate that our HR efforts make business sense, and we provide numbers related to turnover, employee engagement scores and productivity. But the hardest task is quantifying the critical intrinsic value of feel-good culture builders, such as teambuilding, community service events, engagement committees and morale-building effort that are embraced and celebrated by strong cultures.

What we do know is that these "softer elements" continually build into an overall feeling within the organization, and that vibe ultimately drives numbers in a positive and often exponential way. It's a special multiplier effect that strong cultures produce. One of my colleagues refers to it as "all the little prisms (perspectives) within a kaleidoscope" that create the beautiful image. I love that in so many ways.

Here's one such story: our engagement committee had been planning a trip to the Free Store Foodbank. We secured approval from our CEO, granting everyone a half-day off in order to attend (again, in a billable environment this is a very big deal). After months of planning, we were excited to don our matching t-shirts and make the trip to help hungry children who wouldn't otherwise get weekend meals.

A few days before the big event, I had a conversation that would forever change me. My boss, who we will call George, was in a state of panic as I walked into his office. He was in the middle of a discussion with a new hire but wanted to ensure we spoke about this important issue at hand. He was speaking very loudly, and I could tell he was agitated, spewing, "How are we going to take half the company offsite for half a day event when we're not meeting our quarterly numbers? This just isn't going to work! I really don't see how we can do this."

Altruism be damned, we needed to meet numbers. George and the C-Suite were extremely stressed over this. Similar to Tom Cruise's outburst in Jerry McGuire, "Show me the money!" George said, "Melanie, I need you to show me the numbers! How is the company going to benefit from attending this event?"

I explained that this trip was a morale-building, feel-good event to give back to the community and to remind our team that we are a company that cares about others. It was part of the greater good and bigger story that we were creating within our culture. Sculptors of our own culture. I tried to help him see that we can't always produce a hard number that will directly impact profitability.

George proudly offered this alternative, “I have an idea...let's get a temp agency to hire people who we can send to work at the Foodbank.”

As he spoke, George outlined an imaginary triangle with his finger on the palm of his left hand and continued, “The Foodbank gets workers, people get jobs, and we get to keep our team billable to clients! And we meet our quarterly numbers... so everyone wins! We'll call it a triangle of happiness."

Speechless. I looked intently at his face to assess if he was serious, and the sad truth of the matter, he absolutely was! Again, I explained that while it's difficult to put a number on the event, it was good for our team. It was also weeks in the works, teammates had planned it into their week (to get important client things done around the time out of the office) and, moreover, it needed to happen. At this point not having the event would have been catastrophic to morale. As I left his office, he was still shaking his head in discontent.

He yelled after me, “You still didn’t show me the numbers!”

The big day of the event came and went, and our team had an amazing time. We worked together to create meals for more than 2,500 children, took pictures, shared laughs and had a great team-building experience. I was so proud of what we accomplished, and I hoped that leadership would be too.

Later that night as I was driving home, I received a call from George. He was very quiet (which is unlike him), he took a big breath, paused and then simply said, "You were right."

I paused. And smiled.

And responded, "Can you please show me the numbers?"

To which he was gracious in his reply, "No, you were right; it does *feel* good. The team was so engaged. This event will be memorable for a long time. I guess you *can* teach an old dog new tricks!"

It was a moment that greatly impacted and defined me ever since. Sure, numbers matter but not solely or without concern for the intrinsic value of building into a team at a deeper level. Numbers can be calculated (lower turnover, higher productivity, improved efficiency, more engaged customer service – all leading to company profit) even as you focus on the softer elements (fun, engagement, learning, morale, communication and more) of your strong culture. Culture is a positive multiplier, and this Foodbank story is a great example of this.

Later that year we went on to win our coveted, "Best Place to Work" Award. And in the end, the numbers proved that we stayed the course in a good way with engagement scores, morale, performance and retention. Sometimes you can't see the improvements happening (or measure them); you just have to believe and stay the course of the plan.

When leaders focus on all of the THRIVE™ Model areas, they are covering ground to ensure all essential areas are working in your favor and toward a holistic culture plan. Retention happens in a variety of ways, but most importantly, it's founded in how we treat others. Good people stay when good leaders provide a framework for good things to happen. Lay the framework, work your plan and continue down the path of retaining your team.

> *"Coming together is a beginning, staying together is progress, and working together is success." – Henry Ford*

Personal Application

Just as we apply the THRIVE™ Model to our business, we can apply these areas to our personal life as well. How do rewards and recognition show up regularly in our personal life? How are we showing appreciation to others (friends/family)?

We live in a society where abundance is seems second nature. Often times we have so much that a true reward is rather infrequent. If we want something, we just buy it. Many Americans have no idea what it is truly like to need for basic things. We have Amazon Prime on speed dial, and we get frustrated when a package doesn't arrive within 24-48 hours. Our society demands immediate gratification.

Before making that next purchase, stop and ask yourself if this is something that I truly *need* or is something that I merely *want*? Often the answer will surprise you. Simply placing the item in the cart and waiting a few days can often stop the temptation of making an impulse purchase. It's a good practice that I try to remember myself.

Rewards and recognition matter because they are motivators in life. What motivates people to do what they do? One might argue that personal upbringing and intrinsic (within themselves) beliefs are the foundation of motivations and spur us forward into action.

But can we motivate others externally? Can we prompt them to take action? With words, objects or actions of our own? For example, my family is an external motivator for me to hold a job, make money and provide a house, but this is founded on the internal motivator based on the desire to be successful.

> *"Light a fire under their ass." – David V. Rains*

This saying reflects Dad's belief that you can get someone motivated with strong words, arguably this might not be the best way and may lack tact. Don't worry, dad, I will love your passion to motivate others to get them going. But not everyone was brought up with a 280+ pound principal (who no longer had his paddle at school because paddling students was not allowed, however it was a great threat for your own children) to keep their butts in line.

That's more of a stick approach than dangling the carrot. Let's focus on the positive reinforcement side. How would you want to be recognized by your friends and family as a means of showing appreciation? And what is a meaningful reward? Often times receiving a simple "thank you" can mean the world to someone.

There's a book called *The Five Love Languages: How to Express Heartfelt Commitment to your Mate*[11] by Dr. Gary Chapman which I highly recommend reading. Chapman outlines five ways that people express and receive love: through positive affirmations (words), gifts, acts of service, quality time and physical touch. These are pretty self-explanatory, so I won't go into great detail (again, check out the book), but this is the communication/DISC equivalent of learning how to show appreciation.

For example, my love language is "Acts of Service." My husband could shower me with gifts, but he'd be wasting money. Nothing says "I love you" more than when he empties the dishwasher, goes to the grocery, or helps with the laundry. Now that's appreciation, support, understanding and love all wrapped in one big service blanket! When we are showing appreciation for others, we need to consider how they best receive it – not how we prefer to give it. (There's also a workplace version of this book called *The Five Appreciation Languages*. They use the same foundation but ensure that it is work appropriate. This would be a great read to help hone your skills in showing appreciation to others in a way that is meaningful to them.)

> *"I could pinch your ears to the bone." – David Rains*

Ok, so that's not medically appropriate wording as I think there's only cartilage in there. Regardless, dad showed love and appreciation with a gentle pinch of the ears. Three pinches accompanied by a hum for each pinch, and then he'd always ask us, "What does that mean," and we knew it meant, "I love you." It's his greeting and his farewell, and sometimes it happens just because. He's not afraid to show emotion, even the dogs get their ears pinched. Dad will often complain about earrings getting in the way of his expression of love, but even earrings can't deter his ear-pinching intentions. And now, having kids of my own, of course I pinch their ears. My dogs' ears, too. I guess it's a family tradition now, and it makes my heart happy when my son runs to Papaw as we greet them and always goes right for the ears. Love and appreciation – don't be afraid to show it.

"The family that _ together, stays together" – David Rains

(Most commonly the word "prays" is used in the blank and it rhymes nicely, but dad always gets great joy changing the phrase. He adds any word that he wants: plays, eats, laughs, farts, etc. So, I guess we could take one out of dad's book and say: "The team that __ together, stays together" which would be a great mantra for retention!)

Reflection Page: Retention Matters

What should we START doing to ensure Retention Matters?

What should we STOP doing to ensure Retention Matters?

What should we CONTINUE doing related to Retention?

Other Important Notes:

7

IMPROVEMENT MATTERS

THRIVE™ Model usage: Improvement Matters

Start at the foundation/roots, laying the foundation for improvement includes:

- *Personnel Files:* Developing basic files and processes for security, confidentiality and administration of your personnel files.

- *Record Retention:* Ensuring you have procedures in place for basic record retention timeframes for employee files, forms and tracking mechanisms.

- *Performance Reviews:* Creating an entry-level performance review system so that employees will get feedback on a regular basis related to job performance.

- *"Do it All" Mentality:* Wearing many hats is the norm, and leaders get pulled in multiple directions. This stage involves doing whatever is needed go get things accomplished. When organizations are just getting started (or don't have the size/budget to pay for additional hands-on deck), this is how it has to happen.

- *Basic Safety Plan:* Developing a fundamental safety plan or checklist to ensure that safe practices are on the radar. This might include a few bullets in the handbook and essential/required training, a basic safety plan exists but is not very robust at this time.

- *Exit Interviews:* Listening to feedback is important to improve efforts, and leaders can learn a lot about gaps and areas for where we need to do better. Ask the tough questions upon departure of teammates (whether in person, through a 3rd party, or with an online survey). Learn from the feedback and make improvements accordingly.

Once you have this foundation, you can move upward into the growth opportunities/branches:

- *Technology (HRIS) Driven*: Most importantly, it is a Human Resource Information System for tracking and reporting functionality. Some organizations use a Human Capital Management System (HCM) which does similar things as the HRIS, but also links together other applications (Payroll, Learning Management System, Customer Management System, etc.) Gone are the days of massive excel spreadsheets that are cumbersome to maintain. Embrace technology – it's our friend.

- *Digital Processes:* Utilizing technology to support the processes you've already created. Tech will help streamline for efficiency and overall productivity. This could take the form of automated payments, electronic signatures, web applications for bookkeeping, or using a scanner to minimize paper storage. Don't be afraid to ask around to see what tools others are using to make life easier.

- *Coaching Culture:* Motivating your staff and not talking down to them, leaders ensure there is a proactive coaching culture that occurs in real time and not just on a scheduled (annual) basis. Leaders will stop using words like "Probationary Period" and adopt more positive language like "Evaluation Period." Coaching discussions are part of how you communicate and do business every day.

- *Strong Partnerships:* Willing to ask for help, instead of a do-it-all mentality. Leaders are confident in their role and know their expertise. Then, they bring in subject matter experts to train, lead projects and fill in the gaps. Strong partnerships pave the path to get things done with known leaders in their field. These might include a good business coach, a recruiter or a consultant to get to the projects that you just can't seem to tackle. Think of this as the new form of delegating – get expert help and let them make you look like a rock star.

- *Safety Culture and Committee:* Moving beyond a basic safety checklist, you aim to instill a safety culture. Leadership ensures that safety planning and behaviors are critically import, training is always prioritized and a committee with cross-departmental participants is created to ensure that is the case.

- *Stay Interviews & Surveys:* Moving beyond just exit interviews, now our team is focused on proactive feedback while employees are still engaged and working. Take the time to gather input from the team, look for trends in data, and ensure that action is taken to make improvements. Communication will be critical here, to ensure that voices are heard and feel respected – but also knowing that not every piece of feedback can be acted upon. Leaders should be transparent to the extent possible. Your team will value being able to voice their opinion on business matters, which will improve morale.

When we do these things, we ensure that IMPROVEMENT within our business matters. We are building a foundation, making important choices, working our plan, engaging in strong habits and are on our way to becoming a great place to work, leaving a culture legacy that will make us proud. When people matter, cultures THRIVE™.

> *"The dictionary is the only place that success comes before work."*
> *– Vince Lombardi Jr.*

Continual incremental improvement is a requirement in today's workplace.

This section of the THRIVE™ Model is intentionally broad so that it can be a catchall for any areas that we may not have specifically addressed.

Don't get me wrong, I'm a big fan of improvement; however, it's also important to remember not to let perfection get in the way of progress. I like to encourage leaders to aim for 1% better every day (or week), and then imagine how great we can be in 1 year. Let's explore some of the ways we can improve matters with or organization.

First and foremost, a change mindset is needed. Moving forward *without* one gets us stuck in a rut and is a sure path to business decline and employee turnover. While change can be difficult for some, it's a necessary evil to ensure that organizations don't grow stale and complacent.

As teammates challenge the status quo and find new ways to get things done, job satisfaction and productivity will increase, and your organization will be propelled forward. Strong leaders will push for those forward-thinking ideas and reward behaviors that support a change mindset so that employees know the organization supports change and encourages it. We must allow mistakes without punishment as long as teammates learns from them.

Training and Development

A focus on training and development is one of the best ways to develop yourself or others within your organization. At times we have to jump through the required hoops to ensure that we have mandatory training completed (anti-harassment, legal hiring, etc.). Even in these types of training topics, there are great lessons to be learned and golden nuggets to be gleamed.

Get your team involved in their learning. Ask about their desires for improvement in coaching discussions and during performance reviews. Set goals for training and development throughout the year. Be sure to make educational moments ones where people participate and share experiences so that the learning sticks. Don't let sitting still be an option.

Keep in mind that training and development at its core is also about improving ourselves as people. It's hard to separate the two because if you are learning and growing, it's happening personally and professionally. One does not operate without the other; that's the glory of bringing our whole selves to the table at work /home. It's pretty amazing that employers have the ability to make people better (as long as they are willing and able participants). Don't squander that opportunity. Build others up, and they will build the organization up along the way.

> *"Bring your whole self to work. I don't believe we have a professional self on Monday through Friday and a real self the rest of the time. It is all professional and it is all personal."* – Sheryl Sandberg, COO, Facebook

Technology

Technology is our friend, and we need to make good use of it. Companies that embrace technology are climbing the improvement ladder; we cannot sit idly by and miss the bus on this.

Simple processes often start off with a paper process (such as personnel files for record retention), and as the organization grows, so does the need to go digital. Efficiency is key, and paper shuffling is cumbersome.

Keep an open ear for systems that are being used in order to make life simpler with digital means. An HRIS and/or HCM are not scary – as they take pride in being user friendly. Usually, you can get started through your payroll provider, utilizing their tracking and reporting system for employees. Start with this and grow from there, adding features as needed and as you become more proficient using the tool. Your vendor should help you learn how to use it best, and there's plenty of online knowledge being shared (Google it!) if you are uncertain. Performance reviews, training, hiring, payroll and benefits enrollment – there are a multitude of systems to there to take these digital.

In case you haven't heard: superteams are here to stay. What is a superteam? A study from Deloitte[12] brings this terminology forward, indicating that it's when artificial intelligence (AI) technologies partner with humans. Using technology as a tool makes people more productive and efficient. If we don't want machines to take over our jobs, we must learn how to leverage and utilize tech as a competitive advantage. Forward thinking companies use AI to guide people in making decisions. When these technologies are integrated with humans, we can enable teams to use their complementary skills, re-architect work in more human ways, and pursue new and better outcomes at greater speed and scale.[23]

Leaders and teammates must utilize new technology and AI to ensure systems are efficient. Everyone must fight the desire to stay in our comfort zone and learn to embrace technology as a friend. Don't be afraid, everyone has a learning curve. Know that in time, utilizing technology will set the organization apart from the competition.

Employee Surveys

Another critical way to make strategic improvements: let employees have a voice. Our recent survey of HR leaders showed that only 50% are conducting engagement surveys of their team, and of that, the minority were using an *independent third party* to assess the data and make neutral recommendations. Whether they are exit interviews, stay interviews, pulse surveys or bigger engagement surveys, take time to ask for improvement ideas. This is a game changer. Often leaders/HR are too close to see the forest for the trees.

If you really want to know how other organizations are doing things, partner with a strong culture coach to discover new perspective and ideas related to other organizations. Benchmarks only exist when we compare ourselves to outside sources. Your coach can also engage and mentor leadership to uncover new ways of thinking in order to make meaningful changes.

There are organizations that exist solely with the intent and purpose to help your organization do better. Fractional support (with consultants / coaches) can be obtained through an independent consultant or through a company like RCSN, People at Your Service (PAYS) or The Business Hospital, who employ a plethora of consultants/coaches. Partner with a strategic connector who can direct you to the best fit for your organization's needs.

Why does improvement matter? Because when we work toward improvement (of ourselves, our work or our company), we are altering our momentum in a positive way and the result is improved performance. As we look forward and focus on improvement, recognize that everyone has an opportunity for learning and growth.

Change isn't always easy, but it's needed. Improvement matters, and your team will value that your organization wants to get better and values the new perspective that change brings with it. Whether that's improved mindset, technology, understanding our why, or personal/professional development – taking steps towards improvement guides us down a better path for stronger workplace culture.

> *"Standout performance correlated to affirmative responses to these five questions: Structure and clarity: Are goals, roles, and execution plans on our team clear? Psychological safety: Can we take risks on this team without feeling insecure or embarrassed? Meaning of work: Are we working on something that is personally important for each of us? Dependability: Can we count on each other to do high-quality work on time? Impact of work: Do we fundamentally believe that the work we're doing matters?"— John Doerr*[5]

"None of us, including me, ever do great things. But we can all do small things, with great love, and together we can do something wonderful." – Mother Teresa

***Personal Application*:**

Just as we apply the THRIVE^{TM} Model to our business, we can apply these areas to our personal life as well. How does improvement show up regularly in our *personal life?*

Improvement comes in many forms. Some people will make New Year's resolutions. Others will make vision boards and aspire to make those visions reality throughout the year. Some will write down their goals in SMART form, and others will scribble ideas on their bathroom mirror. Whatever path this means for you, stay on the journey. Keep working for improvement.

I tend to think of improvement as ongoing and take pride in being a lifelong learner. Aiming for 1% better every day is a powerful idea that motivates me toward continual self-improvement.

I'm not saying that it's easy. My kids would gladly offer up my shortcomings (I sometimes lack patience and just might cuss a little too much). But I'm keenly aware and keep striving to get better. My kids don't like it when mommy cusses, so I try to set a better example and find more neutral or even silly words to express myself. I'm consciously working to use other words (the kids like "moose poop" better than "bullshit" ... but it doesn't make me feel quite as good) or suffer the consequences of paying up. The kids happily put out a cuss jar to make money off of mommy's inappropriate words. Amazingly, those sweet conversations tied into a physical punishment do make me stop and think before I speak. Now that's accountability at its best.

"They can take your money, they can take your car, they can take your house...but they can never take your education." – David Rains

Education is a blessing. Pursue it with conviction and passion. Growing up in a house with educators as parents, there was a high value placed on academics and doing well at school. My father's quote above is such a wise comment. As a businessperson who weathered a few layoffs, and even as an entrepreneur who knows business struggles, I always find peace of mind knowing that as a worst-case scenario: I might lose physical items, but I could always start over in a corporate job and my education/degree/credentials/knowledge would always be there to lean on. Of course, my kids now hear this phrase as they grow up. Let's hope that they take it to heart and become life-long learners, too, and then pass this wise saying onto their kids as well.

> *"I've been this way for 72 years, and I'm not changing." – David Rains*

Another common saying from my childhood household, and dad means it! He's always been rather stubborn. Hey, dad - we all need to work on improving ourselves, *even* as we get older (Matt, remind me that I said this when I get older and start reciting dad's wisdom here!).

Part of getting better is listening to other ways of doing things, trying new ideas and garnering new perspectives. I remember when I first attempted to leave my trusted Blackberry for the first models of the touch-screen phone. I unpackaged it in awe and looked for buttons. After a long five minutes of frustration, I quickly decided that I could not give up the satisfaction of pressing buttons. That was how I had always done it before – why change now? I returned the touch-screen phone and got a newer Blackberry.

We all know how that story ends. Eventually, I tried again. And again. Using my iPad helped, and I eventually got used to sliding on screens and the new type of interface. I forced myself to try something that was way outside of my comfort zone. Now it's hard to image going back to a Blackberry (do they still even sell these?). Funny enough, that it feels as antiquated as using a flip phone! And who knows what wonderous technology is lurking around the corner for future users. Embrace the change, keep trying.

Technology can be tricky this way, but it's one area in our lives with continual overlap between personal and professional endeavors. I know technology has made me a better business woman, streamlining things for efficiency and productivity. However, even if I wasn't learning it for myself, I'd be learning it for my kids. To protect them from cyber creeps, to understand their digital world better, to help them login to online classes or just to try to keep up with how quickly our society is evolving in the digital realm. Small steps with continual practice reap big changes and reward. We can do this!

> *"Be patient with yourself. Self-growth is tender; it's holy ground. There's no greater investment." - Stephen R. Covey*

There's More at Stake Than a Game

It's not a secret, but the behavior at our kids sporting events has gotten out of control. Sadly, activities that are supposed to be fun, have turned into a hostile culture for many kids. While coaching my kids in SAY soccer, I experienced part of this sad national epidemic. But it's our kids and student athletes, experience the most impact due to this situation, as they struggle with demonstrations of poor sportsmanship, bad leadership at the coach and board level, an undercurrent of sports bullying and out-of-control spectators.

I found a breath of fresh air – when I was introduced to Lori Carnathan, founder of "*There's More at Stake than a Game®*" (MASTAG). This organization's focus is to put some much-needed perspective back into youth sports and to rebuild the youth sports culture. This mission obviously is near and dear to my heart, since culture and kids rank among my highest priorities. And so I dug in, to find out more about what is happening amid the youth sports culture in America.

Lori tells some amazing stories (some of bad behaviors, other of encouragement) as she pursues this mission with such passion. She strives to get the message out to those who need to hear it most (parents and schools) – and she is right; our children are moldable, shapeable minds and need to know that sportsmanship toward both your team and others is a big part of life – sports is just the training ground.

MASTAG started with a primary goal to promote sportsmanship and educate our community. They create videos (made by students for the community) that have a strong impact and resonate with students, parents and spectators. MASTAG soon realized a bigger opportunity (dare I say responsibility?) to carry this work forward and impact the community at large, starting with youth sports and working through high schools. MASTAG was created to make a difference, and Lori knew she was onto something.

I helped Lori create a program that we could roll out to schools in the area. MASTAG welcomed parents and students to think of other ways to share the movement, be bold and be creative. Simply put, this work within youth sports cannot rest on young minds alone – they need our support and partnership.

The MASTAG movement is intended to be something that schools can utilize year-round and includes a variety of ways to show support and get involved, which includes:

- Signing the positivity pledge - 3P Sign-Off (Pledge of Positivity for Parents)

- Watching and sharing MASTAG videos, repeatedly showing the video in the pre-game warm-ups and online with your community

- Reviewing the "Living Our Mission" Motivational Messages that are sent out each week from MASTAG and talk about the sportsmanship concepts during practices, games and at the dinner table

- Wearing the MASTAG gear – coaches' shirts, warm-up jerseys, hats and more customized to each team

Like any tradition in our community, the things that we repeat gain the most momentum and often have the most meaning. Another example of the power of habit. One person alone cannot change a culture but creating repeatable positive habits can redirect things in a positive way. Many hands, making for light work.

Lori and I crafted some great messages urging others to step up. Reminding them of their ability to be the change agent, whether as a parent, coach, bus driver, referee, teacher, counselor, janitor, nurse, gym instructor, principal or superintendent. We firmly believe that the right attitude and belief system toward youth sports can (and will) lay the groundwork for lasting change and a more positive youth sports culture.

We can elevate the commitment to youth sports reform in a positive way. MASTAG is dedicated to building strength of character, giving the sports back to the kids and getting rid of hateful antics. It's about building student leadership, embracing proactive messaging, and creating public accountability around these issues.

We can ensure youth sports are a positive experience for our kids; schools and youth sports groups can lead the way. Indeed, we are at a tipping point, finally approaching the day when adults and kids alike agree that poor sportsmanship (from any party) has no place, when empathy and kindness are recognized and rewarded and when schools work to equip their students with social and emotional competency.

And more good news (this is my favorite part): the outcome of this work will increase participation, improve mental health, build life-long lessons and friendships and, in the long run, lift test scores and graduation rates. *A strong sports culture will distinguish a school and community as one of excellence.*

As with any great idea, the MASTAG Movement takes time and effort to sustain. Lori and I have found it difficult to keep things going; people love the idea but don't really want to put in the effort to make it happen. Due to the stop of sports during COVID, the MASTAG Movement came to a sudden halt. Our grand plans had to take a back seat to our jobs, health, and kids' online education. But that doesn't mean this initiative means any less in our communities.

There really is so much more at stake than just a game. Our future generations depend on our work in this arena. And so, *I urge you to be part of the change.* Even without an official movement – you can take action to make things better. Find your voice to help within your community: always set a good example at your kids' games, don't yell at referees or coaches, teach your kids to win and lose graciously, always strive to be the better person and build a better youth sports culture for our kids. When we know better, we do better. So, let's collectively do better - our kids future depends on it.

In today's world with so many trials and uncertainty, there's one thing that you can always count on – *yourself*. If we want to improve, we cannot keep doing the same thing over and over and expect different results (we know that as the definition of *insanity*). We must look for areas that need improvement (dare we say change!) and be willing to put in the effort to try to make things better.

Great leaders do not shy away from "that's how it's always been done." No, we look for ways to adjust the sails. We work toward the greater good, coach and align where possible and kick the people off the bus that should probably have never been on the ride with us in the first place. It's not always easy. Change never is. Stay on the journey and keep making yourself better. Improvement matters.

Reflection Page: Improvement Matters

What should we START doing to ensure Improvement Matters?

What should we STOP doing to support Improvement Matters?

What should we CONTINUE doing to ensure Improvement?

Other Important Notes:

Take a few moments to reflect on one of your dreams and then take just one step to advance it.

8

VISION AND VALUES MATTER

THRIVE™ Model usage: Vision and Values Matter

Start at the foundation/roots, ensuring we meet the basic needs:

- *Defined Values and Behaviors (Cards for Culture©):* Operating from the baseline for vision starts with defining your vision and values, ensuring that the entire team understands why you are in business and why it matters to employees, leaders, the community and beyond. Set expectations based on acceptable behavior, coach to this, and hold firm in what you believe in.

- *Understand the WHY:* Compelling others to want to work within your organization is important. Understanding the "why" we do what we do changes the way our team thinks about the work at hand, giving it meaning and making the work more fulfilling. The organizations' strong values show up across the company in our habits and are consistently role modeled by leaders.

- *Open-Door Communication:* Ensuring your organization has open communication is important. Leaders must encourage transparency (appropriate amount with regards for confidentiality) and honesty in communication keep lines of communication open and flowing for the entire team. Employees are encouraged to share their thoughts and concerns, without the worry of retaliation.

- *External Branding:* Understanding that our external marketing casts a wide net to reflect outwardly to customers and the public – leaders must ensure that it reflects the workplace culture accurately. While a website is rather elementary in this phase, the organization should also be culture conscious when creating fliers, recruitment information and other marketing materials.

- *Office Manager/HR:* As we grow, we recognize that Human Resources is an important department to show that we truly value our people. If we are small enough that utilizing our Office Manager/COO makes sense, that's ok, but the organization should invest in a qualified HR consultant to train/coach that person to ensure we are meeting baseline needs and legal requirements.

Once you have this foundation, then you can move upward into the growth opportunities/branches:

- *Lived Values & Behaviors (Play Cards for Culture©):* Leveling-up involves defining vision and values, and then celebrating them (ensuring that they're part of our everyday life, our common language, our habits, our display tactics all around the office, and more). They are more than just words painted on the conference room wall – but our Keys to Success. If we have played Cards for Culture© among our leadership team, we are now working the findings into our other practices/habits. We live our values every day and use them as a gauge for acceptable business behavior.

- *Value Proposition:* Moving beyond understanding the "why", your team also recognizes the offerings provided in return for his/her skills. The value proposition is a promise of value delivery which is communicated, acknowledged, and delivered – and acts as a driver of talent attraction, engagement and retention of quality people. By intentionally building into our business practices, policies and everyday language – we can demonstrate the organization's commitment to employee growth, recognition, well-being. It moves the discussion away from the compensation as the primary focus and demonstrates why your organization has a total work experience that is superior and more fulfilling than others.

- *Customized Communication Plan*: Moving beyond open-door communication, our leaders understand that communication is one of the top areas where gaps occur among the team, and therefore leaders work hard to be proactive in that plan. An emphasis is placed on proactive and strategic communication as a means to improve work flows and decrease misunderstandings. Leaders are very intentional in their messaging, thinking through intended/unintended meanings, and aligning with culture norms. Leaders think outside the box with creative ways to engage our team with internal messaging systems (like yammer, GroupMe or Cerykl - giving a shout out to Tarek Kamil for creating Cerkyl - an awesome customizable communication tool!) to ensure communication to each teammate is a unique experience.

- *Internal Branding:* Understanding that while our external marketing reflects outwardly to customers and the public on the website, our internal employee experience is also critically important to our brand. Leaders desire to enhance the brand reputation in order to attract and retain talent. A strong internal brand reflects the image of the organization as a 'great place to work' in the mind of current employees, candidates and other stakeholders.

- *Third Party/Culture Coach:* Moving beyond our trusted HR

person who handles policy, procedures and such, we are not afraid to use a 3rd-party consultant or coach in order to fill skill gaps. We desire to build our foundation, fill gaps where our skills are not strong, and ensure a neutral party supplements our efforts for things like engagement surveys. We value the knowledge that a subject matter expert brings to the table. To build accountability, we seek out a qualified culture coach to truly be intentional in developing a culture with a plan, strategic sessions, and ongoing intentions to ensure culture is a priority at our organization.

When we do these things, we ensure that the VISION AND VALUES of our business matters. We are building a foundation, making important choices, working our plan, engaging in strong habits and are on our way to becoming a great place to work, leaving a culture legacy that makes us proud. When people matter, cultures THRIVE™.

A great culture is *unique* but shouldn't be hard to replicate, especially if it's well defined and built on solid foundation of respect. Does your team know what vision and values guide their daily decisions? Is everyone rowing in the same direction?

Take a moment to define what matters to your organization. Ask others if you (and your leaders) are walking the talk. Make a commitment to define the behaviors that you expect among your teammates in order to build a strong culture with your organization. Write them down. Live those values and display those behaviors every day. Actions speak louder than words.

Ask your team to pick one word that defines the organization and see what surfaces. Those words that are echoing over and over (*data trends*) are a true assessment of what your teams bring to the table each day. Create a Word cloud with those important words, guiding the way for your team. Those trends and that feedback matter to you, to others and to the organization. Believe it or not, it matters to customers, too.

I like to think of culture as: "What happens when the CEO isn't looking?" Then we must ask: How strong is your culture? Do people come in early and stay late? Do you provide opportunities for balance in their life? Do they work tirelessly to meet deadlines, impress clients and get along with teammates? Are you making culture intentional or allowing it to develop on its own?

> *"If our values say one thing, but our actions say something different, it sends a mixed message to the employees. Which leaves a negative emotional impact. This leads to the wild, wild west and bleeds into our crisis of leadership." - Larry Hawkins II, The Purpose Engineer, The Hawkins Devolopment Group*

Some companies take a Google-like approach and toss a ping-pong table in the office hoping that its mere presence will create a great culture. Is it really that easy? More often than not, the table becomes an albatross with people rolling their eyes every time employees start up a game. That's not good for culture. In fact, the negative effects compound as teammates realize the negative stigma with playing the game. The solution? Don't buy the ping pong table if you aren't willing to give people time to enjoy it. No scarlet letters needed.

One of the strongest components of Vision/Values is related to communication. We must listen graciously, keep the doors open to feedback (how we respond when listening to others is key) and also communicate in a way that others can hear us (not always how we want to communicate is). For example, if we prefer to email but our colleague prefers discussion (live or by phone), then we need to flex and do it her way on occasion. Repeatedly sending emails to someone who is buried by email and/or dislikes email, isn't setting anyone up for success let alone progress. Ask others how they prefer to communicate and make efforts to adjust on your end.

We also need to use radical candor when we are talking with others, which means showing that we care personally and then challenge directly. It's a refreshing approach to speaking straight that resonates in a way that can improve communication both personally and professionally.

Check out Kim Scott's Radical Candor[12] movement on YouTube or the book. I whole-heartedly agree with her stance that it's not nice to ignore bad behavior; we owe it to others to give feedback and help them be better. Not everyone subscribes to this idea, but I love it. Radical Candor is life-altering and culture-changing advice for giving feedback in a constructive way so that others can hear it, and you feel good giving it without sugar coating or beating around the bush in order to get results. I urge you to give it a try, speaking straight (with compassion) feels good.

> *"If you talk to someone more than 10-15 minutes on the phone, then you need to go visit them!" – David Rains*

The insight within this message from dad makes more sense as I get older. When he used to say it, I think he wanted me to keep the phone bill under control and get off the one shared home phone line. Boy how times have changed! As I reflect on what he's actually saying here – I believe dad was emphasizing the importance of staying connected with others and stressing the importance of face-to-face interaction.

Bonus, we have more options now than we ever have before, whether in person, by phone or by Zoom/Teams (this newer tool is here to stay and helps us save time, gasoline, and avoids spreading germs!). We can adjust our communication style in a variety of ways. The challenge is to get comfortable with them all, ask others their preference, and then use them appropriately.

Change should be the norm since culture is always evolving. It's a product of action, reaction and more action. Just be sure that you are taking the right actions to move your organization forward and not backward.

Personal Application:

Just as we apply the THRIVE™ Model to our business, we can apply these areas to our personal life as well. How do vision and values show regularly in our personal life?

Vision. I have created a few vision boards over the years. The exercise was always a good one, and it helped me to focus on the things that I wanted to achieve. Whether or not you create an actual board, have goals for where you would like to be in the next 3, 5 or 10 years out (or maybe even thinking about retirement). Vision helps us pave the path for where we want our life to go. Then we use our time, talent and treasure to build toward that goal.

It wasn't until I started working on corporate culture that I really thought about my personal values and those that I desire my family to bring to the table day in and day out.

As I thought about this more and more, I realized that I wanted to come up with something that my children could remember. Therefore, I went through an exercise where I wrote all of the things that I thought were important to me and my husband (and chatted with him about these ideas too). Next, I began the process of condensing and creating something that was memorable and easily repeatable so that my kids could keep it top of mind. And now in the mornings as we kiss goodbye and they head off to school, I kiss their little heads as they run off to catch the bus and we repeat these sweet words:

> *"Be sweet. Be smart. Be strong. And be of service." – Melanie Booher*

These words carry a lot of meaning – more than just face value. And we talk to the kids about what these family values mean and how these are the values that our family is built upon. What are the behaviors and habits that support these Keys to Success? All of this translated down so that little minds can understand it's how we want our family name to be represented. It's a matter of family pride and sometimes a really good discussion point.

There was a time that my son wanted to tell me a story about how *strong* he was because he was going to "fight all the kids at the playground". Insert eye roll here. OK, son, that's not exactly what mommy meant by *strong*. We mean "mentally strong" or "strong enough to stick up for others who are not able to." Or when I received a call from his teacher, that the male Principal had to go into the boys' bathroom to stop the crazy dance party that my son was leading for all the boys. Standing on top of the toilets. Naked. Shaking his private parts in gyrating dance moves (that I can assure you - he did not learn from me or my husband!). Oh my goodness. No, son – that's not a *smart* move. How might we set a better example for others? Some rules are worth following and others should be challenged. This was not one of them. As you can imagine, our family discussions are always interesting as we talk about living our values and work to mold these little minds.

I would encourage everyone to go through an exercise like this and strive to develop values and common language that resonates with your family. It ensures that we have the important discussions with our kids about their character and how we treat others. And when it's ok to dance on the toilets (or not). Defining our family culture. It will also make your heart happy.

> *"Leaders must get across the why as well as the what. Their people need more than milestones for motivation. They are thirsting for meaning, to understand how their goals relate to the mission." - John Doerr*[5]

People who truly want to measure their goals and results might have more of an interest in setting OKRs (Objectives and Key Results). If you are unsure what these are, check out John Doerr's Ted Talk[5], where he explains the importance and power of developing OKRs. OKR's speak to the intrinsic value of the work itself and are key for providing encouragement along the way, not just the final reward (success/paycheck earned). As you work on the OKRs, you achieve the four OKR "superpowers:" focus, align, track and stretch. Superpowers.

John's suggests that we must measure and do what really matters, which is a mirror of our THRIVE™ Model process for culture – provided in a metric-driven way. Focus on the right things, then align and create understanding with defined repeatable behaviors, stay on track by working these into your habits, which allows your culture to grow and stretch. I love this overall alignment!

Aligning Values with Work

One of my coaching roles is as a Regional Director for a networking organization. I gravitated to this group as a member because of the Givers Gain® mentality, the life-long learning approach, the accountability in entering numbers, the good people that I met at the meetings and the entire essence of helping others achieve success in their business. With all that in mind, it seems that becoming a Regional Director would just make sense so that I could coach and help even more people (impacting more than just my weekly group) to improve their businesses across the tri-state.

However, I didn't jump right into the director role with two feet. At the time, one of my mentors was the leader of this group. I was continually watching and learning from him, in awe of his innate ability to be a networker, leader of events, public speaker and strategic connector, all wrapped into one role and connecting over 45 chapters and 1,200 people around the city. He did this and still always made time to express an interest in my business, to mentor me related to growth and referral-based networking and to think of ways to move my business forward.

What started as business conversations and mentoring conversations turned into a friendship. Soon thereafter, I realized that he was trying to recruit me to be one of his Regional Directors. I was flattered, but the commitment seemed a bit daunting, and I was rather hesitant to see how this would fit into running my own business. Could I handle both? Did I have enough time to not only do both, but do them both well?

One Friday, I could hear an insurmountable level of stress in his voice. He really needed me to step up and take the position. I told him I'd give him an answer soon. Unfortunately, I never got a chance to give him that answer. He passed away the following Tuesday. Just like that, he was gone.

In hindsight, there were glimpses into the factors of his stress (work, health, life – the stuff we all stress about), but, of course, that wasn't the entire picture. He was dealing with medication adjustments that were causing some unyielding mental demons, which changed him. His shoulders slumped a little more than usual, his voice sounded more stressed and his million-dollar smile had faded. It was unlike the person that we all knew and loved.

I recall the moment a few months prior where I had called to check on him. I had noticed during a meeting we just left that he was not himself. His normal energy and excitement were missing, and instead of the exuberant and energy filled presentations he normally provided - he gave a lackluster and gloomy presentation. He looked sad. Or was he overwhelmed? I wasn't sure exactly, but I knew something was terribly off.

I followed up with a check-in phone call. In this discussion, he assured me that all was fine; he was just feeling exhausted and trying to catch up on all of his work. We chatted for a bit, and I made every effort to encourage him. I talked to another member of the Regional Director team who knew him better, and we agreed that something was off. Maybe it was holiday stress? We hoped that all would be better soon.

Knowing all that I know now, I wish that I had done more. I knew something was wrong. I was especially hard on myself, thinking what else could I have done? Why didn't I do more? I wished that I had known his family back then, because I would have surely made the difficult call.

Since I was in the middle of discussions about becoming a director when he passed, I figured that my interest and conversations would likely just get lost in the shuffle. His loved ones were now running the business, and they had bigger things to worry about right now.

His father, who was a prior Executive Director, would re-enter as our short-term leader for the region. He didn't know my desire to help. I wasn't sure of next steps, so I prayed and waited. I didn't have to wait long because within a couple months I received a call. He'd found some notes and information left behind saying that I had "great promise and was the next choice for a Regional Director" role. His words were humbling, touching, and also appealing. This was a path for me to step up and help.

The night his father called to discuss things; my husband gently reminded me, "Remember, you don't have to accept right now. Just listen, express your sincerest condolences and tell him you need some time to think about it." Great – it sounded like a solid plan.

Our conversation was pleasant. I did my best to offer up my condolences. I could sense his heartbreak, but he maintained composure and stayed the course discussing business during the call. When I asked him how I could help, he told me that he wanted to move forward with his son's wishes and was hoping I would join the team as a director. He also said, "I have the *perfect* person for you to attend training with, and you can share a room at the Director training in Columbus."

I asked him who my roommate would be – who is this perfect person? Why of course, it was the new incoming Executive Director, the inheritor of the business. It was a woman I had never met before but was very excited to support. The roommate option was my late friend and mentor's *widow*. I immediately felt a huge tug at my heartstrings. He was making a roommate match, but he was also creating an opportunity for me to support her, to lift her up where possible, and to help her get up and running as a new Executive Director.

Really, he had me at hello. However, the roommate information sealed the deal. I knew in my heart that I needed to step up to help however I could, and this was the path that God had chosen for me (while I'm not usually the most spiritual person, I definitely felt Him urging me in that direction). I accepted the position, "Sign me up for training – where do I need to go?"

I agreed to take on two chapters so I could still focus on growing my HR/culture-shaping consulting business. He was so gracious and thankful, and I knew in my heart that I had made the right decision.

As I got off the phone call, I looked over at my husband. He was chuckling and shaking his head side to side. Knowingly, Matt said, "Well babe, that wasn't exactly listening and telling him that you'll think about it and get back with him tomorrow!"

Nope, it was not. I did what felt right and took the leap of faith. At that point, I didn't want to just be an involved party; I wanted to be an inspiring leader, to support wherever I could and to ease the burden however I might be able. Many hands make for lighter work. And so, I took my first step forward on the director journey.

Two years into my role, I still think about my mentor often. I've become friends with my roommate, our new leader, and now one of my bosses (although the boss part feels more like a client relationship). I hope that somehow, I make her days a little easier when I can. I've increased my role and am now responsible for five chapters. Yes, that's three chapters more than I had agreed to take on, but I've been loving it every step of the way.

When making decisions on how to move forward in your life (work or personal), it's important to ensure alignment with your values and desires. The problem is that many of us haven't taken the time to stop and think about what this means.

If we were to take pause and reflect on what alignment looks like, we'd ask ourselves questions like:

- What makes me happy and eager to get out of bead each morning (everyone needs more of that!)?

- What drives your passion?

- What makes me uncomfortable? (What happens if you lean into it rather than run from it?)

- What things am I saying "No" to that might actually be something I'm missing out on?

- What other things can you add into your life to bring better fulfillment? (For example: community service, mentoring others, coaching your kid's teams, volunteering, making meals for others, visiting the elderly, reading or volunteering at your child's school, the list goes on and on!)

After this personal reflection time, project those positive things that you want to happen into the future. Write them down. Make a vision board.

Envision yourself accomplishing these things and what positive outcomes arise because of it. Tell others about your goals and dreams, which helps create personal buy-in and additional drive for achievement.

Remember, sometimes that right path might not jump out and grab you. Listen to others guidance as they suggest opportunities for you, knowing sometimes they know you better than you know yourself. Continue to say yes to new challenges and building on your experience, even when it makes you a little uncomfortable. Over time, all of these experiences in life will create wisdom, which is absolutely worth sharing.

Doing what you love means that it doesn't feel like *work.* I work hard to be a glass half-full, plenty-of-pie-for-everyone person. I'm aligned with the Givers Gain® mentality, the life-long learning approach, the accountability of entering numbers and the desire to help others so that they can grow their businesses. As I coach, network and help others, the more my cup overflows. True alignment feels good, and I thank my mentor for knowing what I needed, even before I did.

Reflection Page: Vision and Values Matter

What should we START doing to ensure Vision and Values Matter?

What should we STOP doing related to our Vision/Values?

What should we CONTINUE doing related to our Vision/Values?

Other Important Notes:

9

ENGAGEMENT (AT THE TOP) MATTERS

THRIVE™ Model usage: Engagement Matters

Start at the foundation/roots, ensuring we meet the basic needs engagement.

- *Personality Matters:* Engaging teammates at the baseline revolves around the personality of our unique organization. Don't take this uniqueness for granted – it's what attracts others to your cause. Stop and think about what makes your mission/organization different.

- *Involved Leaders*: These leaders are involved in day-to-day work, make important decisions, and think of development/continued education for themselves. Avoiding micro-managers or absentee managers is key, but creating leaders who guide our teammates, communicate transparently and value relationships.

- *Management Developed Goals:* Understanding the expertise and knowledge of our leadership team is important, and thus we give our involved leaders more responsibility when it comes to creating goals for the organization. Eventually the team will have some input, but foundationally this is a good place to start.

- *Organizational Structure:* Developing and communicating an overall structure with an organizational chart (traditional hierarchy or centralized style). The format doesn't matter as much as the clarity that arises from understanding how things are formally structured.

- *Development Opportunities:* Starting to build into our teammates, we understand the need for developmental opportunities, continuing education and required training. There is limited coaching occurring from leaders, often only when required because there is a problem at hand.

Once you have this foundation, you can move upward into the growth opportunities/branches:

- *Personality Still Matters:* Continuing to value the diverse nature of our organization, because our unique personality still matters. We understand what makes our organization different, so we share that with others regularly as part of our common language. We know our strengths and use that as a competitive advantage in the market.

- *Inspiring Leaders:* We're more engaged now, and we move beyond mere involvement toward being more genuine inspiring leaders. We take our leadership role very serious as a role model and ensure that we walk the talk every day. These leaders communicate so that others hear their message in a way that resonates with them. They look for ways to improve themselves and their leadership skills, and more importantly they look for ways to improve employees' skills. Developing others is reflected in the strength of the organization, and these leaders take great pride in building a strong culture.

- *Team Developed Goals:* Leveling-up from management developed goals, we are now getting our teams' input to advance those goals. This increases over all buy-in and spurs performance in the long run. Allowing the team to have a voice in goal setting will help the organization meet goals and thrive.

- *Succession Plan:* More than just having a formal organizational chart, we have moved toward more forward-thinking discussions around what our team looks like without a top-down hierarchical approach. Strong cultures ensure succession planning occurs in order to be prepared for whatever changes happen down the road. It's important to ensure our legacy is in the right hands, knowing that future leaders will continue to build on what we created. Informally structured

- *Embedded Mentors & Behavior-Based Coaching*: Moving beyond developmental opportunities and training, we recognize the importance of coaching our teams. We believe that every teammate should both have a coach/mentor and be a coach/mentor. It's more than just our leadership team who are responsible for coaching teammates; instead, it becomes engrained as a coaching culture. Focusing on the right behaviors that we wish to see repeated is essential within the organization since past behavior predicts future behavior. We have defined those and aligned with our values, and our coaching discussions mirror these values. Coaching culture

When we do these things, we ensure that ENGAGEMENT within our business matters. We are building a foundation, making important choices, working our plan and engaging in strong habits, and we're on our way to becoming a great place to work and leaving a culture legacy that will make us proud. When people matter, cultures THRIVE™.

Engagement is a tricky word. What is the difference between engagement and culture? Sometimes two ideas get lumped together. Wikipedia defines *employee engagement* as a fundamental concept in the effort to understand and describe, both qualitatively and quantitatively, the nature of the relationship between an organization and its employees. Wikipedia defines *culture* as an umbrella term that encompasses the social behavior and norms found in human societies (workplaces), as well as the knowledge, beliefs, customs, habits of the individuals in these groups.

I like to think of it this way: culture is the *behavior* that we see happening and engagement is the way we *feel* about the way things are happening in our company. That's why it's important to address culture; behaviors can be demonstrated, coached and duplicated as part of our habits. Feelings are much more emotional and, as you can imagine, more challenging to replicate and coach.

Engagement is a current buzz word that has gotten a bad rap due to engagement surveys. You know the kind – the ones that are offered to employees to gather their feedback only to never be heard from again as the results disappear into the great abyss. If you want to quickly and surely undermine the credibility and trust of your leadership (or HR) team, mishandle the communication, goal and overall process of an engagement survey. It will forever leave a bad taste in your employees' mouths, and it will not be quickly forgotten. "Remember that time leadership asked us how we felt about ____ (fill in the blank). We gave them input, and we never heard from them again about the subject. "

The handling of an engagement survey needs to be done in a positive and proactive way. We recommend utilizing a neutral third party, so employees feel comfortable being open and honest during the survey without fear of retaliation or raising overt concerns related to confidentiality. A good consultant will advise that he/she is looking for data trends, and can keep most thing confidential unless there's a legal reason to need to share (which usually surfaces as a red flag issues like discrimination, harassment, etc.)

Another important element that often surfaces is related to the communication of the survey itself. It's critical to communicate why are you doing the survey, and that while they may give feedback on a variety of topics, not every idea will be able to be acted upon. Leaders desire to listen and learn from their team, all the while looking for trends in the data. Then after careful analysis, leaders can address ideas and make the best changes for the overall company. Every recommendation will not necessarily result in change. It's important to be forthright about that upfront. This is a great way to be transparent with no surprises.

We've heard a million times that "people don't leave companies, they leave managers." We also discussed this a bit in our Retention Chapter. It's probably something we cannot say enough: organizations today need more than merely involved leaders – they need inspiring ones. Leaders who engage others and are worth following. Leaders worth getting up every day and leaving your family/loved ones for long hours, because they are worthy of your time and talent. Does your organization have what it takes to engage and retain your talent?

Leadership buy-in is one of the biggest obstacles in strengthening a company's culture. If you need stats to drive the point home, consider this: when Deloitte[12] surveyed 3,000 leaders (across 106 countries) and culture/engagement was the largest issue. And while 86% of C-suite believed culture is important, only 45% think something is actually happening to change it.

Almost half of the leaders surveyed didn't think *meaningful action* was taking place to guide a strong culture change. We must recognize where we have gaps and empower our leaders to make the needed changes in order to realize improvement. *And we must do this over and over.* If your organization has leaders who are not taking action, consider replacing those leaders. Spur action and intentionality in shaping the culture that your team wants and deserves. Only engaged leaders should apply.

What should you do when you recognize that a leader is struggling or not the best fit for the organization? As with any employee challenge, first start with building trust, fostering open communication and some level of direct coaching (either from yourself, their supervisor, or through a coach/consultant).

If you are not in a position to lead the charge (maybe the challenging leader is someone above you), then this becomes a little more difficult. In some organizations, coaching up is kin to career suicide. Hopefully, you have an open-communication environment where feedback at all levels (up, down and lateral) is expected and welcomed. If this is not the case, you might consider implementing a leadership mentoring program or training and development opportunity to get leaders talking about areas of improvement. This is a good reason to ensure that even leaders/executives are included in some type of review process, opening the door related to strengths/weaknesses.

Just as we learned in the prior chapter, teammates change over time, so will the coach/leader. If coaching the leader is not successful, whether it's because of an antiquated approach (leaders must be able to compete in today's market) or failure to align with the defined culture, sometimes a new leader is needed. Don't be afraid to make calculated leadership changes. New perspective can be refreshing – all in the name of organizational success.

Being a leader can sometimes be the upmost challenge. How do you remain engaged when you're being pulled in so many directions? This is a fundamental question that many leaders ask themselves, especially when sometimes you just want to go home at the end of the day and bury your head under the covers. What? Show up every day? Yep. A true leader knows they have to get out of bed every day, do the best they can to keep things moving in a positive way and be engaged with their team.

The "secret" to improving engagement in the workplace is that there really is no secret. It's a fundamental building block for a strong culture that starts with asking employees what needs improvement, or the changes needed to be made in order to make their time at work more productive, and helping them feel genuinely connected with others and that their work matters. Engagement starts with listening to what employees want/need. Really listening. Even if that means coaching current leaders to be better.

Top employers have a collective commitment from the leadership team to be authentic, flexible and communicate with clarity. Always building trust, allowing the team to have a voice through surveys, in developing goals, and about important topics as they arise. Ensure that mentoring and coaching goes up, down, and across the organization so that we can continually improve and keep a pulse on our team's viewpoint.

It's the link that must surface regularly between being a good person and bringing that good person to work every day with you. Treat others with respect and value what they bring to the table. These simple solutions should not surprise us. Engagement happens at all levels and is contagious when we allow it to grow and thrive within our teams.

Personal Application:

Just as we apply the THRIVE™ Model to our business, we can apply these areas to our personal life as well. How does engagement show up regularly in our personal life?

> *"I AM the straw that stirs the drink" – David Rains (also Reggie Jackson)*

Dad always says this to signify that he is on the ball, top dog or maybe even kind of a bad ass. Which cracks me up. Bottom line, he's a mover and a shaker. He motivates others and/or gets things done himself.

Engagement at a personal level speaks to the art of showing up on a daily basis. Are you present and engaged with your loved ones? When you sit down to dinner, do you have great conversations, or are you hiding behind a cell phone? Do you listen more than you talk? Do you ask questions to understand what the speaker is saying? Do you show understanding and compassion for others?

Personal engagement is challenging in society today when there are so many distractions to pull us in different directions. It takes great discipline and focus to be fully engaged.

At the corporate level, we talk about the difference between being involved and being inspiring. This applies at the personal level as well. Involvement on a personal level is also very foundational. I can be involved with neighbors and kids sports, but it takes a different level of engagement to be inspiring and motivating your friends/family to be the best they can be on a regular basis. Give your best effort to help out, offer advice and go the extra mile when you are able. Inspiring takes effort and thoughtfulness. Sometimes, inspiring can be tiresome; it's ok to take a break and bring our best self the next time.

Think of someone who has inspired you in your life. What did they do? How did they treat you so that you actually wanted to do better, to do more and to race across the finish line? If you are fortunate enough to have inspiring people in your life, take a moment to thank them and then think about how you might be able to provide inspiration to someone else. Pay it forward to others and bring them up with you. Small actions can get the ball rolling – nudge it forward in the most inspiring way you can.

Engagement Matters Story

I was scheduled to take over as the manager for a new team. I went to a team meeting and met the departing manager in order to get introduced to meet teammates, learn more about the group, and gather some perspective from the out-going leader.

After the meeting, the leader and I decided to grab brunch so that we could discuss the team's areas of success, ideas for improvement and finalize the transition. We discussed teammates, and she gave some background and her very, very negative perspective. She described them as "awful" and went through every person's shortcomings. She advised that my style of being an annoying cheerleader would not go over well, and that I should not "blow that culture sunshine up their ass." Given her negativity, I doubted this group ever wanted to reach out or ask her for help. Her spite was abundant.

Since she was leaving the manager role, I asked for other insights and best practices from her time working with the group. Why did I even venture down this path? I think I was still trying to be polite and make nice conversation. Not my best move. This question opened a floodgate for her to attack my style rather than provide areas where she'd seen success.

She advised that I "needed to shut up and listen to other more tenured leaders and to stop offering my ideas. They've been doing this longer than we've been adults." She told me that my "Polly-Anna approach and new ideas were intrusive," adding: "I didn't talk at a leadership meeting for quite some time." Again, she reiterated that my culture focus was ridiculous.

I'm pretty sure this was the most toxic discussion that I have ever had in my life. She thrived on the negativity and drama of her rant, which she continued for about 45 minutes. Until this point, I had choked down lunch, remained rather quiet, maintained my composure and listened.

I guess that I experienced an out-of-body moment where I imagined myself standing up and saying to her: "Let me show you how Polly-Anna blowing out my ass works!" and I would flip over the lunch table and walk out. Ha. That's not my style. Obviously, that wasn't the right way to handle things. I gathered my thoughts, knowing that I would not allow her to say all these hurtful things without some feedback (or sticking up for myself) on my end. I knew that I'd regret saying nothing; that was not an option.

At a moment of silence, I jumped in to say, "Well, thank you for the information and feedback. I can tell you do not have an HR background or must coaching experience." She asked what I meant by that. I explained how her delirious rant was hurtful and lacked any decorum of respect or professionalism. I knew she didn't have HR background because we think before speaking and consider others feelings. She didn't even seem to understand what was hurtful about her tirade.

All of the challenges that I'd gone through in the past year came rushing to the surface. She didn't know anything about my world, my three medical surgeries or other personal struggles. Being a new manager and this new job was proving to be a positive experience.

I started to get emotional at a time when I really didn't want the other person to know how upset I really was. But I couldn't hide the emotion any longer; something about this conversation hit me like a ton of bricks. I felt myself getting really upset, like knot-in-my-throat-can-barely- speak upset.

I needed to gather myself and get to my next meeting. She didn't want me to drive in such a disheveled state, and it was the first sign of humanity and compassion that I'd seen from her. The distanced and venomous look that I had seen in her eyes lifted. I could tell she felt badly about driving me to tears.

It was kind of a blur after this. She followed me outside the restaurant and was apologizing profusely. Strangely she asked for a pinky swear (I believe this was her hug alternative) to confirm that I was ok to drive. She was turning on the charm and trying to calm me down, but it was too late at that moment. Rather out of character for her, she asked for a hug, of which I obliged out of exasperation (or maybe in an attempt to be the bigger person). I was frustrated with her, but I was frustrated with myself for letting her see how upset I was. It was a strange interaction with a roller coaster of emotions.

I got in the car and sat there for a moment, gathering myself. Trying to understand why I had let someone so toxic impact me so thoroughly and rain on my parade. However, the reoccurring, negative comments about culture that stood out the most. It felt like a direct attack on my life's work, and it was really hurtful.

In a moment of clarity, I realized that this person was not someone I needed to waste my time worrying about. She was not a friend, a family member or a client; she was a soon to be prior co-worker, and our paths didn't need to cross any further. Later, I would continue to reflect to see what I could learn from the situation and how I could handle things better in the future.

If toxic communication and overall negativity is what she had to offer, our team was certainly better off without her. She was moving on and taking a new role, which likely gave her the courage she needed to have such an unpleasant departing conversation with a colleague.

Surprise - her new job didn't work out. Within a few months she called me to "make sure I was ok with her rejoining the team." As if I had a choice? I am the kind of person who tries to learn from things and keep moving forward, forgiving and forgetting and not holding grudges. I appreciated that she called, as I'm sure making that phone call was not an easy one. Before the awkward phone call ended, I asked her if she wanted her "awful" team back. Surprise again, she passed on that invitation.

Fast forward to later months of working with that team. I toned down culture language, but I was myself and continued to lead with respect and civility. I worked to earn their trust and figured out ways to help them, offering support, coaching through difficulties, addressing problems, offering new ideas and providing a consistent positive person to rely on. Working to build trust as their leader.

During a workshop that I conducted for the team, we reviewed their metrics, talked about possessing a positive growth mindset, and discussed adjustments needed to improve the overall business. The team was engaged and listening, they participated when asked questions, and they offered suggestions for improvement. A few teammates stepped up and agreed to help hold others accountable.

Based on this workshop, ongoing team coaching, positive discussions, peer-based accountability and teamwork – the metrics started to improve. What was once the worst report in the organization, now showed signs of improvement. They can only go up from here.

Guess what a little kindness, coaching, and positive support delivers? We started to see positive behaviors and success from the team. They showed up more, participated more, and also met and exceeded earning goals! This caused them to be recognized for their accomplishment, which earned them an award. The change was palpable – and for me it was just really rewarding and exciting to see their team-based success.

Even with these great steps forward, there were still challenges that surfaced around performance and attitude. Through additional support, recognition, and discussions about their success – they have persevered. Why should they continue to step up? Continued success, that's why. They had a taste of what team success feels like and they wanted to keep it going. This is how you build a strong team culture – one step at a time.

Which style of leadership resonated with this group more? Obviously the two styles presented were light years apart. One was the carrot; one was the stick. This is an example of engaging with people and moving beyond directive and distanced leadership with minimal involvement. Leaders must start with a foundation of trust – people don't care how much you know, until they know how much you care. Listen, learn, respect and build trust. Stay on the positive side of things, but don't be afraid to address issues in a productive way. Motivate where you can. Listen to others when they offer blind spot awareness moments, take the feedback and try to be better.

This story is a great example of how engagement and leadership styles matter. Teams need the support of their leader in order to thrive. Never underestimate the power of leading with heart.

PART III

10

MOVING FORWARD

At this point, it's obvious that you are on the "Culture Matters" bus. You've likely read some books, articles and blogs, or you've attended webinars and conferences, and you keep hearing buzz words that remind you of its importance. It sounds like a convincing argument. You want great culture for your company too. Now what needs to be done? Can I do this myself, or do I need to get help making it happen? How do I get leadership on board if culture is not their focus or priority?

Culture-first thinking is showing up more and more, which is the good news. However, we also have noticed that culture enhancement needs an extra nudge in the right direction and a little additional support. Typically, this is because leaders can have the best of intentions, but their plate is full. So very full. And the thought of adding another thing to the plate - well that doesn't go over very well. Here's the thing: culture cannot be another flash in the pan or chasing of the bright shiny object, only to be forgotten the next time a novel idea comes around. Culture will always be important and *should always be a priority.*

The way to ensure your workplace culture doesn't get placed on the bookshelf to grow dusty within your organization is to instill THRIVE™ Model elements into your habits. Ensuring that the responsibility doesn't fall on one person's. shoulders. It's not HR's job to lead culture. Nor the CEO. The responsibility falls on everyone. Thus, the power of habit is key; because once a habit becomes rooted in your life (personal or work), it becomes automatic.

The THRIVE™ Model urges leaders to create the roots first and then build and strengthen that foundation. Continue to build upward, shine light on those areas that need attention, prune others that don't fit and create the ongoing growth that you want to see in the branches.

James Clear has written a book called *Atomic Habits: An Easy & Proven Way to Build Good Habits & Break Bad Ones*[14] which I encourage everyone to read. One of my favorite tactics that I learned from James is the concept of *habit stacking*. To do this, simply identify a habit that you already do each day (like brushing your teeth) and add a new habit that you want to develop to the old one or "stack" this new behavior on top of it.

I used this approach to help me find time to write each day. When I get my coffee, I sit down and write for a bit, even if only 10-15 minutes. More often than not, that 10-15 minutes turns into more time. Thus, the new habit is developed (and in my case, a book is written! Yay!).

The need for a strong culture isn't going away any time soon. Times of turmoil accentuate the need for strong culture as employers struggle to navigate the changes tossed their way. People are facing more adversity than ever, from additional stress at home, to social upheaval and political turmoil, to a global pandemic - and those are just the things we know about. We simply cannot keep piling it on and hope that employees can maintain their same level of productivity and morale.

Yet, with all this happening in the world, people still have a simple desire to enjoy whatever path we choose for ourselves. And for most, it's a path that covers the majority of our daytime hours (ahh the joy of work!). Therefore, the importance of culture is paramount. Our humanity is formed upon this desire for good, where good people deserve a good work environment. Good leaders simply cannot ignore the significance of workplace culture.

It's critical that leaders do what's best for their people. If you have the time and expertise on staff, I urge you to implement some of these ideas/projects internally in order to save money. But more often than not, those who think they know culture don't have a tangible plan beyond trusting their gut and/or being good with people. As we've learned throughout prior chapters, planning is important, but action is the most essential element.

For many leaders, the thought of investing in help to drive culture is unheard of. But staying the course is not a good option either. Usually, I hear that there simply is no budget for something as innocuous as company culture. Given the many ways that culture impacts the bottom line, we must reexamine those beliefs. I'd say NOT investing in culture is a sure-fire way to lower morale, drive performance down, increase absenteeism and turnover, and ultimately drive the organization under.

Be a disruptor. Create your plan, consider ideas/tools to help move culture projects forward in an intentional way but without breaking the bank. And, good news: many things can be done without additional budget. The THRIVE™ Model will help provide an outline to succeed. Start in the roots and add more options to help level-up into the branches.

Here are a few recommendations to help move your culture-shaping forward within your organization:

Utilize the THRIVE™ Model

Obviously, this is my favorite tool. There could be some bias here! This is a great tool to support companies as they make sense of all the things needed in order to build a strong foundation and grow from there. From roots to branches, we are reviewing processes and practices that make our culture stronger. People Operations/Human Resource processes support this journey, as they are main proponents of the areas addressed within the model.

Putting a physical (written) plan in place in order to drive action is the key. Join the less than 10% of companies that actually plan for their culture. The THRIVE™ Model helps leaders do more than just trust their gut.

Construct a plan, garner alignment so that everyone is on the same page, make continual improvements and apply the power of habit. You will see the results in morale, productivity, turnover and more. And it will generate a competitive advantage and ensure a resilient legacy. Bonus: this tool is FREE. Details are outlined throughout this book, and you can print a copy from our website.

Get a Coach / Mentor

Everyone needs a coach/mentor and should also be a coach/mentor to someone else. As leaders progress up the ladder of success, they often stop utilizing professional development (training, coaches, etc.) because we believe that our own knowledge and experience outweigh the contributions of a coach. There is a fallacy of thinking here. Leaders must be willing to listen and learn new things, as we all have blind spots and areas that need development.

The world of being a Culture Coach is a relatively new one, but it's much needed. I have a variety of clients who have happily elected to sign up for Culture Therapy (actually called a Culture Strategy Session) in order to keep their Culture and People plan moving forward, brainstorm new ideas and also hold them accountable.

Personal and business coach/consultants are booming in a big way as everyone strives for ongoing success. Whether you need help with sales, navigating LinkedIn, general direction/success, organization, mindfulness, wellness, conscious business leadership – the list goes on and on – there's bound to be a coach for you.

With so many coaches at hand, leaders should ask for referrals to good coaches, interview coaches of interest, and ultimately find the best one that fits your needs. Through partnerships like RCSN and networking groups, I have coaches of all kinds that come to mind. I've included a list at the end of the book to get you started and I'm happy to make introductions.

Similarly, it's important to find others to mentor/coach as well. Pay it forward. I have been participating in a student mentoring program for HR students at the University of Cincinnati for the last couple of years. Tom Mobley has done an amazing job with that program, and I'm happy to support him and his students. I've been lucky to meet some wonderful students - some of whom I still keep in touch with – and I have pulled a few into HR project work when possible.

In fact, one of my early students became my first intern (Julie Gyure!) with MB Consulting Solutions. We met at the SHRM National Meeting in Washington, DC, a few years back. During that trip we bonded over the Cleveland Cavaliers championship game victory, and we have been friends and colleagues ever since. The joy of watching your student grow up in their HR roles, change jobs and/or get promoted is very rewarding. And what's really cool about this reward is that it goes both ways – both the students and the mentor benefit!

Play *Cards for Culture*©

A new idea for alignment and progress – *Cards for Culture©: The Business Edition*. Some have compared the game to Apples to Apples or Cards Against Humanity but with a culture vibe, but we don't want to set the bar too high! While there are some similarities, our game facilitates a good discussion to help clarify what your culture means (determining *Keys to Success* and *Defining Behaviors*) and how to embed it through habits and tactics (*Bring to Life*) within your workplace. This revolutionary game literally places company culture in your own hands through three different decks of cards.

Even if you already have Vision & Values noted within your organization, most employees can't reiterate them. Memorization is not how the human brain works to recall these things, and more often than not, your cited important attributes are not linked to what your organization is trying to accomplish. Sadly, confusion abounds.

With that in mind, we can help you create that important link! The game is a unique and fun way for leadership teams (any team really!) to build comradery, improve communication, foster trust and align expectations related to organizational culture. Gamification of culture is new and exciting, and it's a critical step in building engagement among your leadership team.

Gamifying culture with *Cards for Culture©* makes it memorable and fun. Bonus: amazing discussions, clarity and alignment will follow. So, gather your top leaders (obtain a facilitator, if desired, to help with time management, defusing situations, and the added benefit of holding accountable) and set aside some time to determine your *Keys to Success*, *Defining Behaviors* and ultimately - *Dring to Life*.

Use Assessments

DISC: One of my favorite tools is the DISC assessment, and Mark Allen is my go-to-guy for getting these done. DISC is a great tool to help you better understand your communication style and the style of those around you. It provides insight to help you understand the "how" behind the "why" when it comes to communicating with others. Once you understand how you are perceived and how others like to be communicated with, you connect at a much deeper level. If you are a team leader, team member, sales professional, or entrepreneur you will see better results when you understand and apply this tool.

What I really like about DISC is the fact that many people are aware of it, have taken a DISC assessment and have an idea of what their personality style is. The kicker and multiplier for DISC, is to really take the time to understand how you can adjust your style to better work with others and help you understand them better as well. Taking the assessment but letting the information grow old isn't a good recipe. Flex that DISC muscle, post those DISC profiles at your desk, share with your team and keep talking about how you relate to others. Improved communication and leadership development is sure to follow.

For more information on DISC and to complete a Management Skills Assessment, visit https://markallen.focalpointcoaching.com/

E3/Management Essentials: Our behaviors dictate the results we achieve in the boardroom and the dining room. Understanding how we behave is the first step toward improving our results. The E3 Behavioral Assessment is an effective, simple, scientifically validated, cloud-based tool that measures key behaviors and motivators. It consists of selecting adjectives that represent your preferences and only takes 5 – 8 minutes to complete. E3 scores you in everything from aggression to support, criticality to creativity. Results for key performers create benchmarks to evaluate candidates. Results for teams or organizations define the behaviors which represent an organization's culture. For at its core, culture is the way things are done.

Go Digital

Technology can make culture progress even easier – if it appeals to your team. New ideas are continually popping up in the tech world, so it's hard to keep up with all the ways you could go digital. I've found a few that I really enjoy and wanted to share those with you here:

Dulead is software that serves as your (Virtual) Director of Leadership and Development. Think of it as the answer to the whole "Now What?" question after completing organizational assessments and engagement surveys. It implements a playbook of the best practices required to align, develop and retain your people, and it takes care of it for you automatically and continuously over time.

CultureWise has a great app that businesses can use to automate culture reminders, quizzes, letters from leaders and more. It takes your defined culture and ensures your fundamentals are right in front of your team on a regular basis. I highly recommend checking this out if you work with a tech-savvy group who always has their phones in hand and would embrace this technology-based approach.

Utilize Strong Partnerships

We cannot make culture change by ourselves. Nor can we get all items in the roots/branches accomplished without assistance. Take a moment to inventory which things you feel comfortable working on and are within your wheelhouse. Then select a few projects that would be good to supplement (outsource!) and bring in a SME partner.

Specific organizations are listed in the Partnerships/Links section to help you get started. As always, reach out if you'd like help with introductions to any of these organizations.

Become a Certified Culture Coach / Leader

We are excited to announce that aspiring culture leaders (geared toward Human Resource Leaders, Business Leaders, and Independent Consultants) can now get certified as a Culture Coach!

Our culture certification network is a group of elite, hand-picked, heart-rooted leaders who really want to make a difference and take culture to the next level either within their own organization or consulting for others. The program will teach you the ins/outs of what we have learned about culture-shaping over 20+ years, accumulated from many industries, leaders and approaches. We will provide applicable coursework designed to teach the comprehensive THRIVE™ Model methodology, provide examples of templates and processes to build into your workplace, and *also* pair you with a network of other culture coaches to expand your resources and support.

Additionally, our THRIVERS have access to 1:1 coaching, roundtable discussions with other culture leaders, plus additional guidance and mentorship as needed to answer questions and ensure your success. After completing this certification, you will have the tools and knowledge needed to build a THRIVE'ing culture and help your organization become a best place to work. Not to mention the elite talent that you will start attracting!

*SHRM PHR credits will be available upon completing this certification.

11

FINAL THOUGHTS

Culture is not rocket science; it's investing in people because good people are the heart of great organizations. Those good people need a plan and support, which I've outlined through an abundance of ideas mentioned here and structured by the THRIVE™ Model). Believe in your team but also take action. Give them tools to level-up and construct habits to make living the values of the organization second nature. And then leaders can build the culture of dreams. But better- making dreams a reality. (My quirky mind feels there's a reference here to *Field of Dreams*... "If you build it, they will stay").

Throughout the US, and hopefully beyond - we are amidst a humanity movement. Challenging situations (like the pandemic) surface feelings of isolation, indifference, fear and sadness. For some, work is the escape they need from personal chaos at home. For others, work is just something they do to pass the time until they get to be with loved ones again.

If organizations want to be competitive in their respective markets, it's essential to ensure the organization's culture is part of the competitive advantage and that it shines. We can do this by being intentional and utilizing the THRIVE™ Model's six key areas and new ideas for action to help guide that intentional strategy. Being purposeful in the culture we desire to create.

Remember, *"Rome wasn't built in a day" – David Rains*

We cannot do everything at once. Gradual improvement and culture building takes time and continual focus. Commitment to the cause. If repetition helps us learn, then I am beating the culture drum repetitively: "Build a plan and work the plan!"

We cannot simply hope for the best and trust our gut. We know too much about the importance of a strong culture to be that naïve. And when we know better, we can do better.

Hopefully, you now have a better understanding of why culture matters. I've provided thoughts from leaders, an outline and a heat map (the THRIVE™ Model) that can be your foundational culture plan. I've applied our learnings to personal situations and pulled in stories to help us understand where the rubber meets the road. I've provided new ideas and recommendations for partnerships that can help you move things forward. All of this wrapped in the fundamental idea that there's a deeper connection between the good people who foster the strong cultures and the great workplace culture that we so desire.

Our personal and professional lives are intertwined because we are human. We care about work and family. We want to be good people and deserve to enjoy our workplace, too. It's up to us to ensure that people matter and to get the snowball rolling so that it grows and grows. This book reminds us of our part in making the world what we want it to be.

Like Trevor in the *Pay It Forward*[2] book, we must take the assignment seriously: "THINK OF AN IDEA FOR WORLD CHANGE AND PUT IT INTO ACTION."

Are you ready to be part of a movement that will change lives for the better? Here, in our immediate personal surroundings, in organizations, within our state, our country and around the world. The power lies in the momentum of a few strong leaders, building culture, leading with respect and creating great places to work. Just imagine all of the employees who can be positively impacted and their families/loved ones who they go home to at night, experiencing this good person/great culture movement. They are happier, more engaged and more connected.

Positivity is contagious. It starts with making the choice to be better. Embracing the day ahead of us. Making the right choice, time and time again. Even with it's difficult to do so. Asking ourselves: What do we want to be known for? What kind of legacy do we want to leave behind? We answer these questions with conviction and a plan to do better. We make the conscious decision to be a good person, good leader and leave an amazing culture legacy.

This book is the first step, sharing it and encouraging leaders to take steps forward. Baby steps if needed. Just keep moving forward. And we can grow beyond our roots, beyond the leaves...the sky is the limit. Exponential growth. Culture is the multiplier.

Given your choice in leisure time and obvious good taste in books (this one!), it's clear that you are already part of this culture-shaping movement. Culture is a collective commitment that is bigger than any one of us. We can pay it forward so that everyone gets the culture they deserve. We can leave the world a better place than we found it. One good person, one game plan and one great work culture at a time.

And so, we take action so that our legacy can be one of Conscious Culture (good people, creating great work environments to spur a great culture movement) and knowing that: "*Together We THRIVE*™."

CONNECT WITH US

This book was written so that you can take things in your own hands and build the culture you want for yourself. Taking small steps to build a strong culture – good people/great culture movement growing from the desire to make positive changes by those who are willing to persevere.

We are here to support you if you need it. Please reach out if you need additional inspiration, coaching, guidance, guest speakers, connections and/or workshops for your business.

Join our culture movement to ensure strong workplace culture is the priority that it needs to be - and together we can change the world.

Ways to connect:

Website

LinkedIn

Twitter

Instagram

Facebook

Calendly

PARTNERSHIPS & LINKS

Culture by Design[4]**, Fundamentally Different**[3]**, High Performing Culture** were all part of my CultureWise learning and partnership. Allow me to introduce you or check them out here: www.culturewise.com

E3 Behavioral Assessment

As a bonus for investing in Conscious Culture, please take the E3 Behavioral Assessment for free (a $250 value) by visiting: https://bit.ly/3u3vdnP

You'll receive an email with a series of links to your key behavioral attributes, critical growth areas and motivators. These brief, concise, actionable recommendations will allow you to understand how you're leveraging your key behaviors as well as learn what you can do to keep them from becoming the best version of yourself. www.MgmtEssentials.com

Focal Point Coaching & Training – Mark Allen

Business coaching services will help you to understand and implement proven business concepts, strategy and tactics that are guaranteed to generate rapid Return on Investment. Mark will coach you to develop effectiveness in key areas related to achieving this success, including: Strategic planning, Profitability and Growth, Leadership and Team Building, Management Effectiveness, Productivity, Execution, Exit Strategy. His value to clients is provided in several ways including: one-on-one coaching, group coaching, topic specific training, and behavioral assessments (DISC) and financial assessments.

https://markallen.focalpointcoaching.com

Give to Get – Jonathan Mardis

Rethink the job transition and recruitment experience. GiveToGet (GTG) is an exclusive community-based organization that is "Revolutionizing the Job Transition World" to bring exceptional leadership-level talent together with value-centered companies. This is a community of employers, talent, career consultants and connectors. We cannot wait for you to be part of the revolution! http://www.givetoget.us

Human Resource Fractional Support / Consulting Firms

I am a firm believer in partnering with a great Human Resource to support your needs and help get projects completed and pushed over the finish line. Supplementing your HR team is a proactive and forward-thinking choice. Some of my favorites include: A Slice of HR, Aliniti, RCSN, and strategicHR.

PayOptions – Janelle Paynter

They focus on the underserved small business client (1-100 employees) and are unique due to their dedicated service model. PayOptions offers clients customizable technology with 1-1 personal service (you have a representative that works on your business, not just a 1800 number to call). They go above and beyond to bring the highest level of service at the lowest possible price. Website: www.payoptions.com

RCSN – Paul Wehner

RCSN is a Leadership Services & Executive Recruitment organization. It is made up of a great group of coaches, consultants and recruiters who help leaders improve their overall business performance through: Executive recruiting and recruiting research, Sales, leadership and communication skills coaching, HR consulting (including diversity and inclusion), Culture development and strengthening, Professional development for leaders, and Outplacement services. www.rcsnleaders.com

Reset – Kendra Ramirez

Need a reset? Check out the community that my friend/colleague Kendra has created. Empowering you to live limitlessly. Reset is a mindset community that serves through group coaching masterminds, monthly lives, and online courses. Bringing you coaches and stories of people who have reset their mind and proving you can too. Your current mindset can stop you from fulfilling your dreams. When you are in a better headspace, things begin to fall into place. Reminding you: that you are uniquely and wonderfully made. TheReset.co

The Business Hospital

The only Business Hospital of record in the world. Specializing in the business approach to company health, our assessments, diagnosis and treatment plans include increasing the health of companies by way of organizational strategy, corporate execution and overall effectiveness. We assist startups to large corporations with goal attainment and sustainability. We have practitioners in tech, commercialization, business strategy, sales, fundraising, leadership, human resources and manufacturing. www.jcbaker.org

Turn Leaf Consulting (Peak Productivity & Performance) – Elisabeth Galperin

Providing lasting, life-changing results for highly-driven business leaders who seek greater control of their time as well as effective and efficient use of their talent. Serving as a consultant, coach, and accountability partner, we ensure continued improvement for clients in organization, productivity, and profitability. The clients we serve best are entrepreneurs & business leaders who: have the ideas and the drive needed to create successful businesses; recognize the value of creating and implementing processes & systems to best manage their valuable time; desire creating productive environments in which to work & live. turnleaforganizing.com

---

This is just the tip of the iceberg for quality providers who can help you move things forward related to people, HR, and culture needs. Visit our website at www.thrivewithmb.com and submit a "contact us" form for a free discussion and partnership introduction.

"That's all she wrote" or *"Goodnight, Irene!" – David Rains*

Kind of like "boom, end of story." Thank you, dad, for all your wonderful insights. I smiled a bunch while including these golden nuggets within the book. Hopefully people understand the links and our humor, otherwise we will just wink and laugh together. I love you more. MB XOXO

"Talent Matters"

- Hybrid Workforce
- Talent Management System
- Recruitment Partnership
- Applicant Tracking System
- Behavior-Based Interviews
- Referral Program
- Stellar On-Boarding Process

"Health (of Business) Matters"

- Culture Deck
- Atmosphere & Workspace
- Developmental Training
- Engaged in Personal Life
- Inclusive Community
- Holistic Wellness Plan

"Retention Matters"

- Above & Beyond Benefits
- Market-Leading Comp/ Incentive Plans
- Meaningful Appreciation
- Owner-Minded
- Engagement Committee

"Improvement Matters"

- Technology (HRIS) Driven
- Processes Digital
- Coaching Culture
- Strong Partnerships
- Safety Culture & Committee
- Stay Interviews & Surveys

"Vision Matters"

- Lived Values & Behaviors (Cards for Culture)
- Value Proposition
- Customized Communication Plan
- Internal Branding
- 3rd Party / Culture Coach

"Engagement Matters"

- Personality Still Matters :)
- Inspiring Leaders (Develop Others)
- Team Developed Goals
- Succession Plan
- Embedded Mentors & Behavior-Based Coaching

"Talent Matters"

- Traditional Workforce
- Defined Hiring Process
- Recruitment In-House
- Application / Offer Letter
- Interview Guides
- Background Checks
- Basic On-Boarding Checklist

"Health (of Business) Matters"

- Handbook
- Required Postings/Training
- Job Descriptions
- I-9 Process Created
- Emergency Contact Form
- Diversity Awareness/Training
- EAP

"Retention Matters"

- Basic Benefits
- Competitive Wages
- Rewards & Recognition
- Team-Minded
- Fun Events

"Improvement Matters"

- Personnel Files
- Record Retention
- Performance Reviews
- "Do It All" Mentality
- Basic Safety Plan
- Exit Interviews

"Vision Matters"

- Define Values & Behaviors (Cards for Culture)
- Understand the WHY
- Open-Door Communication
- External Branding
- Office Manager / HR

"Engagement Matters"

- Personality Matters
- Involved Leader (Develop Self)
- Management Developed Goals
- Org Structure
- Development Opportunities

ENDNOTES

1 Christine Fruechte, "Why honing your company's culture should be a top priority in 2021," *Fast Company*, December 28, 2020.

2 Catherine Ryan Hyde, *Pay It Forward* (New York: Simon & Schuster, 1999).

3 David Friedman, *Fundamentally Different* (Philadelphia: Infinity Publishing, 2012).

4 David Friedman, *Culture by Design* (Philadelphia: High Performing Culture, 2018).

5 John Doerr, "The OKR TED Talk," What Matters, March 2, 2019, www.whatmatters.com/articles/ted-talk/.

6 Vern Dosch, Wired Differently (DPZ Technology, 2015).

7 Caitlin Flanagan, "Matt Lauer's Woman Problem, *The Atlantic*, November 5, 2019.

8 Ivan Misner, "Givers Gain® is Transformational," BNI, November 20, 2020.

9 David Perlmutter, Austin Perlmutter and Kristin Loberg, *Brain Wash: Detox Your Mind for Clearer Thinking, Deeper Relationships, and Lasting Happiness* (New York City: Little, Brown Spark, 2020).

10 Teresa Amabile and Steven Kramer, *The Progress Principle* (Boston: Harvard Business Review Press, 2011).

11 Gary Chapman, *The Five Love Languages: How to Express Heartfelt Commitment to Your Mate* (Chicago: Northfield Publishing, 1995).

12 Kim Scott, *Radical Candor: Be a Kick-Ass Boss Without Losing Your Humanity* (New York City: St. Martin's Press, 2017).

13 Junko Kaji et al. *The social enterprise in a world disrupted; Leading the shift from survive to thrive* (Deloitte Insights, 2020).

14 James Clear, *Atomic Habits: An Easy & Proven Way to Build Good Habits & Break Bad Ones* (Garden City: Avery, 2018).

THANK YOU to all who have supported and inspired me!

- MB

Made in the USA
Middletown, DE
01 April 2023